—

AQUACASIA

A collection of simple
and inspired recipes from
the Indian Ocean

—

'THE OCEAN IS CALLING AND I MUST GO'

INTRODUCTION

The Indian Ocean is the warmest in the world. Its scattered islands and continents are blessed with the rich soils and clement climates that gave birth to the spices that changed our world. And our lives.

Spices have been cherished as food flavouring as well as being essential in cosmetics, incense and more from as far back as 3500 BCE. There are Egyptian records of the labourers building the great pyramid of Cheops being fed spices from Asia to give them strength and cassia and cloves from Indonesia, essential items for embalming, fetching high prices.

In later years, particularly in Europe, the use of spices in food came to be the most popular, especially pepper. Spices preserved and, more significantly, made the poorly preserved almost palatable by masking any unappetizing hints of decay. There was never enough pepper to go around, however, and it, like many spices, was quite literally, worth its weight in gold, with 'Peppercorn Rents' being just that. The value of a pound of nutmeg in the 14th century was set at seven fat oxen.

With Arab traders and the merchants of Venice making vast fortunes from the spice trade into the mid 1400s, the Europeans were desperate for a route of their own to the fabled spice islands of the eastern Indian Ocean. It was the Portuguese who knew best how to navigate the unknown oceans and thus, on May 21, 1498, Vasco da Gama and his no doubt relieved crew landed in Calicut having performed the first direct sea voyage from Europe to Asia.

The floodgates were opened and, if the modern age of human history has a beginning, then this was it. In one fell swoop Europe's ignorance of and isolation from the culture, cooking and commerce of Asia was ended forever.

It was a two-way exchange however. The Portuguese kindly brought chillies from their excursions to South America (called 'pepper of the Indies' by Columbus) to India and Asia and later tomatoes and potatoes. These European explorers may have failed in their attempts to convert the locals to Christianity but succeeded in revolutionizing the kitchens of India, Thailand, Indonesia and China.

In addition to chillies, the Portuguese brought 'Carne de vinho e alhos', or pork cooked in wine vinegar and garlic. Local cooks in Goa reinterpreted the dish by using a vinegar made from tamarind and throwing in lots of spices, especially chillies. Thus vindaloo, a corruption of vinho e alhos, was born, and with it a new traditional Indian food. Curry, as we now know it, has become one of the most internationally enjoyed foods on the planet, from Japan and Bolivia to New Zealand and New York. In the latter, a stretch of Lexington Avenue that boasts several restaurants doing a brisk trade in kosher curries has jokingly become known as Curry Hill.

Although it originated in India, curry is not actually Indian at all but a British invention. Early British traders learned from the Portuguese to misuse the word "carree," for sauces made from butter, crushed nuts, spices and fruits that were then poured over rice. In various South Indian languages, "karil" or "kari" referred to spices for seasoning or to dishes of sautéed vegetables or meat and eventually, the word evolved into a catch-all.

It is these intriguing origins and influences of food that have fascinated me for over four decades. An infatuation that has drawn me to every corner of the world and down many a back-street where a waft from some happy Mama's home kitchen has beguiled me with its fragrant mystery and promise.

Cooking, for me has always been an adventure steeped in tempting possibilities. A simple voyage of discovery, where the savouring and especially the sharing of one's brave efforts is perhaps the most natural, deep-rooted human delight possible.

You too can become a 'kitchen traveller' by following the paths we have trodden throughout the islands and continents of the Indian Ocean. It is a vast region, where the tyranny of distance has created many distinct and localized tastes, encouraging each culture to develop and adopt the foibles and flavours of its immigrants, conquerors and visitors, and cooking up a cornu-copia of culinary delights from very much similar ingredients.

For me, ultimately, the fascination is not that these cuisines are so similar but that they are so delightfully different! I am intrigued at how the local plants and fish combined with the inescapable influences of the Arabs, Portuguese, Indonesians, Chinese, Malays, Indians, Dutch, French and English, have been cooked up, absorbed, tweaked, chewed and swallowed or spat out. Creating a unique culinary tapestry woven with fla-vours, techniques and twists that are beholden to and dictated by the fresh, dried and pickled produce that is readily available (and affordable) right now! This is a cuisine born of pragma-tism, blessed by spices and embellished by love.

"Aquacasia" is the term I have coined to refer generally to this exotic Indian Ocean cuisine. The book itself offers you recipes for more than 60 dishes taken directly from the kitchens of the people who have lived on these islands for generations. The recipes might be amazing but they all very approachable, not over fancy or too demanding. Most importantly, they are authentic examples of home cooking collected and perfected by chef Willibald Reinbacher. They look and taste just like the ones eaten and enjoyed by the islanders and they, as 'transla-tors of the place', are the experts after all.

From a Mauritian perspective, with Africa to the west, Asia to the north, Indonesia to the east, and Australia down under, Aquacasia brings together each island's particular love of food wrapped in the culinary art of its people, always with an eye to where it all started.

We invite you to take a magic taste bud ride with us and very much hope that you will enjoy your journey in the cooking and the eating and sharing as much as we have enjoyed ours in the gathering. And never forget: *"Our lives are not in the lap of the gods, but in the lap of our cooks."* Lin Yutang

Bon appétit ...
MPS Puri, Nira Hotels & Resorts

'I AM CONSTANTLY SURROUNDED BY INSPIRATION'

~ Willibald Reinbacher ~

We spent the day with Willi and his team. It gave us a chance not only to peek over his shoulder in the kitchen and see the sparkle in his eyes as his vision was transformed slowly into the reality of the the dish he was preparing, but also to watch him inspect and taste fresh regional produce and chat to the locals at the island's colourful markets. The day simply did not seem long enough for him and left us wondering what are the forces that drive Willi The Restless.

Willi, how long have you been on the island? I've been travelling around the Indian Ocean since 1995. I discovered Mauritius in 2001 and instantly felt a connection there, but it took me nine years to get established on the island.

When were you inspired to create this book? I'm a classically trained chef, but my fascination with other cultures and what people love to eat has been with me for as long as I can remember. All my life I've felt this urge to find the key to a certain taste or smell, and it would keep me awake at night, until I cracked the secret. In a sense, I was a curator of all these wonderful recipes over the years but never introduced them to my guests. While working on this book, I realized that this is more than just a long-lasting love affair with the people, their cultures and their food; it also became clear to me that I'd only just started scratching the surface of this unbelievable culinary richness. Over time it began to surface organically and reveal its beauty. I think I have had "Aquacasia" within me for a long time.

How does someone curate recipes? Yes, it sounds a bit like being an art collector, doesn't it, although I've never seen myself as one. To me food is many things, but not an art form. The taste of our mother's milk is probably the first thing we humans learn to appreciate!

Remember when your mum cooked your favourite dish, or the enticing aroma that emerged when you were walking past the local bakery? All these memories fill you with comfort. And this is precisely where my interests lie: in real food. To me, real food comes from families, from the streets, from markets, from a little diner at the port or a beach shack. These dishes are easy to follow and cook for practical reasons. They alert my senses and have me reach for my notebook. I am constantly surrounded by inspiration! This is how I travelled through the Indian Ocean and this is how I discovered "Aquacasia".

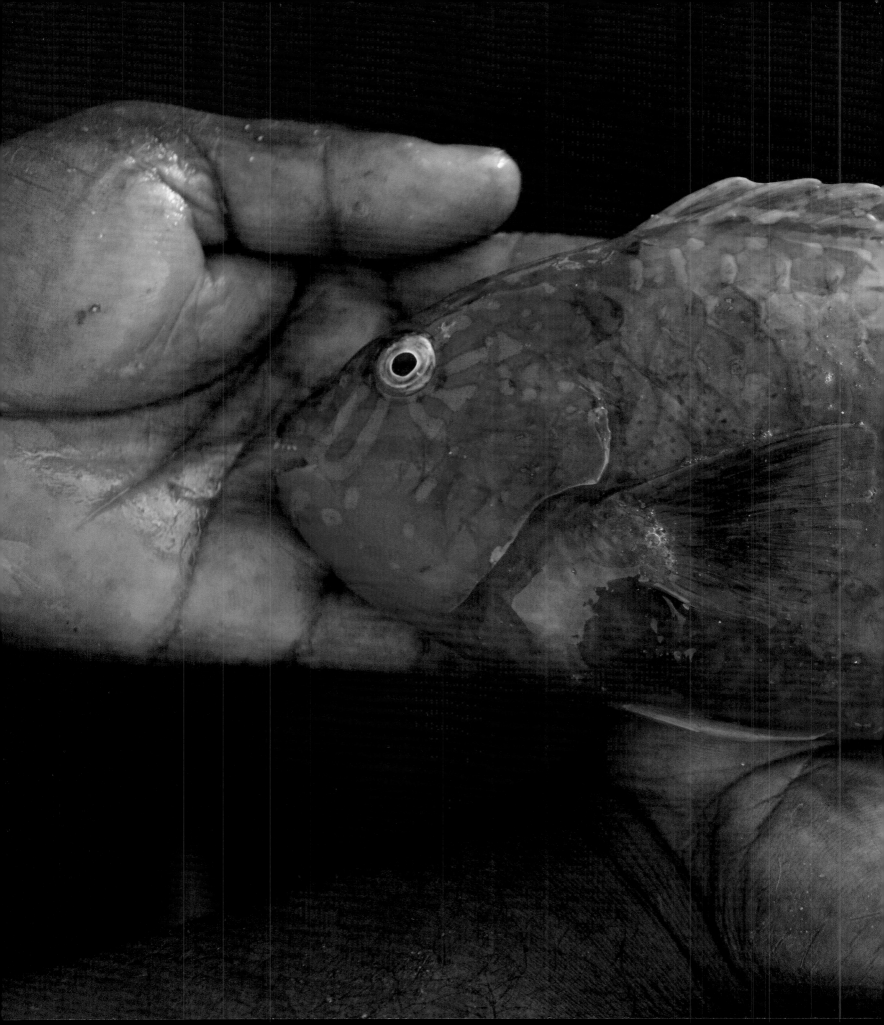

FISH & SEAFOOD

'GIVE A MAN A FISH AND YOU FEED HIM FOR A DAY

TEACH A MAN TO FISH AND YOU FEED HIM FOR A LIFETIME'

~ Maimonides ~

'MANY MEN GO FISHING ALL OF THEIR LIVES WITHOUT KNOWING THAT IT IS NOT FISH THEY ARE AFTER'

~ Henry David Thoreau ~

It is remarkable that so many men are keen to go fishing, yet seem to care so little about the landscape. While they may not merely be in it for the catch – there is adventure in it – their appreciation of nature is often quite small and vague.

Should you ever have the opportunity to go on a fishing excursion with a local fishing crew, don't hesitate for a second. An experience like this is more than an adventure, far more than just a memorable day where you'll get some great pictures to instantly share with those sitting back home. It is a spiritual experience, becoming one with nature.

The fishermen gather at dawn and quietly ready their tools: rods, nets, knives and ropes. Everything is loaded onto the boat. Each task accomplishes precisely what it is supposed to do. Not a single word is spoken. It feels like meditation.

The captain steers his boat towards the shallow spots inside the reef. He sets course to retrieve the traps, navigating directly to the spot where he left them the night before.

There is no buoy to mark the spot – nothing whatsoever, except his instinctive skills. While the men empty their traditionally crafted traps and examine the catch, another crew member puts on his mask and quietly disappears into the water, to resurface a few minutes later with a large, proud smile on his face. He beckons us to follow him. Though we try to impress by copying his elegance when jumping into the ocean, we fail dismally. The fisherman guides us towards the reason for his smile. A few seconds later he extracts a large octopus from a small hole in the reef. The octopus was less than amused, changed his colours, squirted ink and put up quite a fight. But in the end Goliath won.

Back in the boat they chatted about their catch and the problems that confront them with the changes in our ecosystem. For all that, they all seem as happy as sandboys. The sun rises and we all feel at one with the elements.

Like I said: it's a spiritual experience.

LANGOUSTE
À LA VANILLE
COMOROS

YIELD
4 servings

LEVEL OF DIFFICULTY
Medium

TIME
1 hour, 30 minutes

TAGS
Bake, gluten-free, grill

CONTAINS
Dairy, garlic, seafood

While the food of the Comoros is strongly influenced by Arabian, Asian and European cuisine, there is one ingredient that is unique to the island: vanilla.

The fertile volcanic soil enables vanilla plants to grow almost anywhere. Families have naturally incorporated this delicious flavour in their cuisine, and "Langouste à la vanille" is one of the national dishes.

CHEF'S NOTE
Adding fresh green peppercorns to the vanilla sauce lends additional flavour.

SERVE WITH
Steamed rice

INGREDIENTS
4 langoustes (800–1,000 grams, 1.7–2.2 lb each: crayfish (crawfish or spiny lobster)
100 grams (1 cup) **mirepoix** (roughly chopped mixture of onion, leek, carrot, celery)
1 teaspoon whole black peppercorns
3 bay leaves
5 vanilla pods, cut lengthwise
3 tablespoons cooking oil
30 grams (2 tablespoons) **white onion,** chopped
15 grams (1½ tablespoons) **garlic,** chopped
15 grams (1½ tablespoons) **ginger,** chopped
100 ml (½ cup) **dry white wine**
70 ml (⅓ cup) **cooking cream**
50 grams butter, cold, cut into cubes
1 lime, squeezed
Salt and **pepper**

TO FINISH
Salt and **pepper to taste**
50 grams (1½ cups) **baby spinach,** washed

PREPARATION
Cut all 4 langoustes (crayfish) lengthwise, starting from the head. Remove the tail from the head and place to the side.

To prepare a flavourful shellfish stock, heat the oven to 200° Celsius (390°F).

Remove the heads and roast in the oven for about 30 minutes until red in colour. Place the heads in a casserole pan, add the mirepoix, peppercorns, bay leaves and fill with water until all is just covered.

Scrape out the seeds from the vanilla pods and set aside for later. Add the scraped-out vanilla pods to the stock and simmer for about one hour to infuse all flavours. Strain the stock through a fine sieve.

To make the vanilla sauce, heat the oil in a saucepan. Sweat off the onion, garlic and ginger. Quench with the wine and then add the home-made stock and bring to a boil. Reduce the liquid to around 100 ml (½ cup). Add the cream and using a handheld immersion blender mix the butter cubes into the sauce. The texture should become creamy. Add the vanilla seeds, lime juice and season to taste.

To finish the dish, season the langouste tails with salt and pepper and grill on a BBQ until half cooked. Remove the flesh from the shells, cut into bite-size pieces, add them to the sauce and cook gently until done. Stir in the baby spinach and serve.

SASHIMI TUNA SALAD WITH A LIME, SOY AND SESAME DRESSING

VARIOUS ISLANDS

YIELD
4–6 servings

LEVEL OF DIFFICULTY
Easy

TIME
25 minutes

TAGS
Raw

CONTAINS
Fish, sesame, soy, wheat

The yellow fin tuna [Thunnus albacares] is native to the waters of the Indian Ocean. Its juicy meat and fine taste make it very popular with the locals.

Native fishermen still use pole and line fishing methods to catch these very strong and fast (up to 50 miles per hour) swimmers, making it a fair game in comparison with commercial fishing.

CHEF'S NOTE
You can use salmon instead.

DRESSING
20 ml (1½ tablespoons) **soy sauce**
1 teaspoon dashi
20 ml (1½ tablespoons) **lime juice**
40 ml (3 tablespoons) **mirin**
1 teaspoon grated **ginger**
1 tablespoon sesame oil

TO FINISH
300 grams (10.5 oz)
yellow fin tuna loin, sashimi cut
Soy sprouts, chopped
Spring onion, thinly sliced
Sesame seeds, toasted

PREPARATION
Heat the soy sauce and dashi in a small pan and boil gently until the dashi is dissolved, then let cool.

Add all the remaining dressing ingredients.

To finish, slice the tuna and arrange on the plates. Spread soy sprouts across the tuna, drizzle a bit of dressing over it and finish with the sliced spring onion slices and sesame seeds.

WHITE FISH AND
COCONUT CEVICHE

AUSTRALIA

YIELD
4 servings
LEVEL OF DIFFICULTY
Easy
TIME
1 hour, 20 minutes

TAGS
Gluten-free, make ahead,
raw, one-pot meal
CONTAINS
Chilli, coconut, fish

Ceviche is a traditional Peruvian speciality, using the acid of citrus fruit to cure raw fish. In Australia, ceviche is prepared with the iconic barramundi [Lates calcarifer]. Barramundi – named by the Aboriginal Australians – have a mild tasting white flesh. They are simply perfect for this great dish.

CHEF'S NOTE
Alternatively, you can use fresh tender fish fillets such as sea bass, sea bream or fresh prawns and lobster.

INGREDIENTS
200 grams (7 oz) **white fish filet,** thinly sliced
50 ml (3½ tablespoons) **coconut cream**
50 ml (3½ tablespoons) **lime juice**
30 ml (3½ tablespoons) **mild honey**
50 grams (⅓ cup) **red onion**, sliced
1 tablespoon sliced **red chilli**

TO FINISH
1 tablespoon coriander (cilantro), chopped
Salt and **black pepper to taste**

PREPARATION
Combine the coconut cream, lime juice and honey in a medium-sized bowl.

Add the fish, onion and chilli. Cover and let the ceviche marinate in the fridge for at least one hour.

To finish, add the coriander and season with salt and pepper to taste.

PRAWN CURRY WITH COCONUT AND BILIMBI

SEYCHELLES

YIELD
4 servings
LEVEL OF DIFFICULTY
Easy
TIME
1 hour

TAGS
Gluten-free
CONTAINS
Chilli, coconut, garlic, mustard, seafood

Bilimbi is a close relative to the carambola (also known as star fruit) but differs in its appearance.

The long bilimbi is very common, sour in taste and used for "achaar" (South Asian pickles).

In this recipe we use it to lend a healthy portion of acidity to the gravy.

CHEF'S NOTE
If you cannot find bilimbi in your local speciality food store, you can substitute the dish with tamarind paste. Omit the curry leaves if you cannot find them.

SERVE WITH
Steamed rice

INGREDIENTS
12 giant prawns, peeled and without the head (120 gram, 4 oz per portion)
1 tablespoon turmeric powder
1 tablespoon coriander powder
1 teaspoon cumin powder
4 tablespoons coconut oil, divided
½ teaspoon mustard seeds
3 grams (ca. 15 pieces) **curry leaves**
100 grams (½ cup) **red onion,** chopped
30 grams (2½ tablespoons) **garlic,** chopped
30 grams (3 tablespoons) **ginger,** chopped
1 teaspoon red chilli powder
100 grams (½ cup) **tomato,** diced
400 ml (½ cup) **coconut cream**
2 tablespoons peeled, chopped **bilimbi**

TO FINISH
1 teaspoon garam masala
½ lemon, squeezed
Salt to taste
Green chillies, fried

PREPARATION
Mix the turmeric, coriander and cumin powder in a small bowl. Season the prawns with salt and a little of the spice mix.

Heat three tablespoons of the coconut oil in a "karai" (Indian-style wok) or a saucepan and fry the prawns for one minute. Remove the prawns from the pan and set aside.

Add the remaining tablespoon of coconut oil, and when heated, fry the mustard seeds until they pop, which releases their flavour. Add the curry leaves, onion, garlic and ginger, then stir-fry gently. Add the remaining spice mixture and chilli powder and stir-fry for a minute to release the flavours.

Add the tomato and keep stirring until it reaches a paste-like consistency.

Add the coconut cream and bilimbi, then simmer for 10 minutes. Finally, return the prawns to the curry and cook until they are done.

To finish the curry, season it with the garam masala, lemon juice and salt to your taste. Garnish the dish with the fried chillies.

SOUPE DE TECTEC
CLAM SOUP

SEYCHELLES

YIELD
4 servings

LEVEL OF DIFFICULTY
Easy

TIME
45 minutes

TAGS
Gluten-free, soup

CONTAINS
Garlic, seafood

The tectec is a clam found close to the reef in shallow sandy places. Women and children can be seen collecting them at low tide. The tectec (or pipi) are traditionally used to make soups, stews (rugai) or even curries.

The most popular dish in the Seychelles is "Soupe de Tectec" which is proudly served in local restaurants.

CHEF'S NOTE
There are some variations where cooked rice is added. This creates a thicker consistency – similar to congee.

SERVE WITH
Baguette

INGREDIENTS
400 grams (14 oz) **tectec clams** (Seychelles clams or use any other type of clams or mussels)
3 tablespoons cooking oil
70 grams (½ cup) **red onion,** finely chopped
20 grams (2½ tablespoons) **garlic,** finely chopped
20 grams (2½ tablespoons) **ginger,** finely chopped
50 grams (⅓ cup) **tomato,** diced
50 ml (3½ tablespoons) **white wine**
600 ml (2½ cups) **tectec clam stock** (will be made in the process of cooking the clams)
2 sprigs thyme
2 bay leaves

TO FINISH
Salt and **black pepper to taste**
2 tablespoons finely chopped **parsley**

PREPARATION
First boil the tectec clams gently in about 700 ml (3 cups) of water until they open. Drain and retain the water as the clam stock for the soup. Quench the cooked clams in iced water. Clean the clams in more fresh water to make sure no sand remains.

Heat the oil over medium heat in a soup pot. Sweat off the onions, garlic and ginger. Add the washed clams and tomato. Then deglaze the pot with the wine.

Strain the home-made clam stock to remove the sand. Add the thyme and bay leaves and simmer gently until the clams are tender. This depends on the quality of the clams, the ones we use need approximately 10 minutes.

To finish, season the soup season with salt, pepper and the parsley.

MAS RIHA
FISH CURRY
MALDIVES

YIELD	TAGS
4 servings	Gluten-free
LEVEL OF DIFFICULTY	CONTAINS
Easy	Coconut, chilli, fish, garlic
TIME	
30 minutes	

Skipjack or yellow fin (ahi) tuna are traditionally used for this dish. In the Maldives, I preferred using other fish fillets such as grouper or cod.

There are many different ways to make "Mas Riha" (fish curry), but coconut milk is indispensible. In this recipe we use a green curry paste made with cassava leaves [Manihot esculenta]. If not available, fresh wild garlic leaves [Allium tricoccum] can also be used.

CHEF'S NOTE
The green curry paste (page 105) goes well with chicken or – as a vegetarian variation – with vegetables.

SERVE WITH
Steamed rice

INGREDIENTS
400 grams (14 oz) **white fish fillet,** cut into 8 pieces, each 50 grams
30 ml (2 tablespoons) **coconut oil**
5 tablespoons chopped **onion**
2 tablespoons chopped **ginger**
1 teaspoon chopped **garlic**
100 grams (½ cup) **green curry paste** (see page 105)
100 ml (½ cup) **stock** (fish or vegetable)
100 ml (½ cup) **coconut cream**

TO FINISH
Salt to taste
Coriander (cilantro), chopped

PREPARATION
Heat a medium soup pot with coconut oil over medium heat and sweat the onion, ginger and garlic.

Add the **green curry paste** (see page 105) and fry for around five minutes.

Add the stock and coconut cream, then bring to a boil. Lower the heat slightly and cook until it reaches a nice creamy consistency.

To finish, add the fish and cook for a few minutes until it is done. Be sure not to overcook the fish.

Season to taste and garnish with the coriander.

FIHUNU MAS
GRILLED FISH
WITH SPICE RUB

MALDIVES

YIELD
4 servings
LEVEL OF DIFFICULTY
Easy
TIME
45 minutes

TAGS
Bake, gluten-free, grill
CONTAINS
Coconut, chilli, fish, garlic

Every Maldivian family has their own secret spice rubs for grilling fish.

The lime and the refreshing, yet powerful and bold flavour, make this my favourite recipe. Use a skewer if you want to grill the fish like a local.

CHEF'S NOTE
This recipe is good for grilling or roasting any fish. If you catch a large whole fish, adjust the cooking temperature and time to ensure the fish is cooked through before getting charred on the outside.

SERVE WITH
Sweet & sour salad (see page 133)

SPICE RUB
100 ml (6 tablespoons) **coconut cream**
50 ml (3 tablespoons) **lime juice**
1 white onion, chopped
5 garlic cloves, chopped
1 tablespoon chilli powder
1 tablespoon cumin powder
10 curry leaves
3 tablespoons black peppercorns

FISH
4 pieces whole fish, each approx. 300 to 400 grams (10–14 oz)
1 lemon, sliced
1 bunch thyme
Several cloves garlic, peeled

TO FINISH
Chilli peppers and salt to taste

PREPARATION
First make the spice rub. Blend all spice rub ingredients in a food processor to make a paste. Pay attention to the amount of chilli powder you prefer to add.

Gut and scale the fish. Cut shallow slits into the skin of each fish. Stuff them with the lemon, thyme and garlic.

Marinate the fish generously with the spice rub.

Arrange each fish on a wooden skewer and grill until done.

Or arrange them on a roasting tray and bake in a wood fired oven or in a 200° Celsius (390° F) preheated oven until done.

TAMARIND-GLAZED TUNA
MALDIVES

YIELD
4 servings
LEVEL OF DIFFICULTY
Easy
TIME
30 minutes

TAGS
Gluten-free
CONTAINS
Fish, mustard

There is a large Indian influence on Maldive cuisine, which, however, tends to be lighter and based on fresh fish.

Tamarind – the fruit of the tamarind tree tastes fruity, sweet and sour. The fruit is used in many variations to flavour dishes, as a sauce or chutneys.

CHEF'S NOTE
If you cannot find curry leaves omit them.

SERVE WITH
Sweet & sour salad (see page 133)

TAMARIND GLAZE
1 tablespoon cooking oil
2 teaspoons mustard seeds
2 teaspoons coriander seeds
2 teaspoons garam masala
50 ml (4 tablespoons) **tamarind paste**
50 ml (4 tablespoons) **water**
3 tablespoons sugar
2 limes, squeezed
Salt and **black pepper to taste**

TUNA STEAK
4 tuna steaks 150 grams (5 oz) each
Salt and **black pepper to taste**
Tamarind glaze (from above)
1 tablespoon cooking oil
8 curry leaves
1 lemon or lime

PREPARATION
Heat a frying pan with the oil and fry the mustard seeds until they start popping. Add the coriander seeds, garam masala and fry gently for another minute, making sure it does not burn.

Add the tamarind paste with the water, sugar and lime juice. Cook until the sugar dissolves and the glaze reaches a syrupy consistency.

Season with salt and pepper, strain through a sieve and let cool.

To finish, season the tuna steaks with salt and pepper and rub with the tamarind glaze.

Heat the oil in a frying pan. First add the curry leaves and fry them until fragrant. Place the tuna steaks in the hot oil and fry for approximately one minute on each side, until the outside is crisp and blackened, but the inside is still rare and tender.

Season with salt and pepper and serve with lemon or lime.

LA SOUPE
DE CRABE

MAURITIUS

YIELD
4 servings
LEVEL OF DIFFICULTY
Easy
TIME
45 minutes

TAGS
Gluten-free, soup
CONTAINS
Garlic, seafood

Fresh water crabs are often found in waterways near the sea. They leave their dens with heavy rains and high seas. That is when local fishermen harvest them.

Sometimes the crabs caught are too small, so they feed them until they grow large enough to sell on the market or to enjoy themselves.

CHEF'S NOTE
If you prefer a spicy version – add some chopped chilli when sweating off the vegetables.

SERVE WITH
Baguette

INGREDIENTS
400 grams (14 oz) **crab concasse** (crab in shell, cleaned and cut into pieces)
5 tablespoons cooking oil, divided
100 grams (⅓ cup) **white onion,** chopped
30 grams (2½ tablespoons) **garlic,** chopped
30 grams (3 tablespoons) **ginger,** chopped
2 teaspoons thyme, chopped
50 grams (⅓ cup) **carrot,** diced
50 grams (⅓ cup) **celery,** diced
50 grams (⅓ cup) **leek,** the white part diced
150 grams (¾ cup) **tomato,** diced
1 teaspoon turmeric powder
800 ml (3⅓ cups) **vegetable stock** or water

TO FINISH
Salt and **pepper to taste**
Coriander (cilantro), thin slivers

PREPARATION
Heat a soup pot with half of the oil over medium to high heat. Fry the crab until well roasted and red in colour. Remove the crab and set aside.

Heat the other half of the oil over medium heat and sweat off the onion, garlic and ginger. Add the thyme, vegetables, tomato and turmeric, then stir-fry for approximately five minutes until all becomes fragrant.

Add the vegetable stock or water, bring to a soft boil and cook until all ingredients are soft for about 20 minutes or longer. You might have to add a little of water if you simmer over high heat as the water evaporates.

To finish, return the crab to the soup, reheat the crab, season with salt and pepper, garnish with the coriander and serve.

OCTOPUS
VINDAY

MAURITIUS

YIELD
4–6 servings
LEVEL OF DIFFICULTY
Easy
TIME
1 hour, 30 minutes

TAGS
Gluten-free
CONTAINS
Chilli, garlic, mustard, seafood

Indian workers brought dishes and practices to the culinary traditions of Mauritius in the 19th century, such as the extremely popular "vinday". It is best with fish or octopus.

SERVE WITH
Steamed rice

INGREDIENTS

600 grams (1.3 lb) **octopus**
2 tablespoons cooking oil
2 tablespoons mustard seeds
2 tablespoons sliced **garlic**
2 teaspoons turmeric powder
4 medium-sized green chillies, halved lengthwise
2 teaspoons whole grain mustard
100 ml (½ cup) **red wine vinegar**
200 grams (2 cups) **red onion,** cut into thick slivers and separated by layers
200 grams (1½ cups) **capsicum** (bell peppers) **of mixed colour,** cut diamond-shaped

TO FINISH
Salt and **pepper to taste**

PREPARATION

Clean and wash the octopus thoroughly, removing the hard centre. Rub it with some salt and rinse with cold water.

Place the octopus in a saucepan, cover with water and bring to a boil. Lower the heat and simmer for approximately 30 minutes until tender. Let the pan cool down, remove the octopus from the water and cut into large pieces.

In a frying pan, heat the oil over medium heat, add the mustard seeds and fry until the seeds start popping. Add the garlic, turmeric powder, chilli and stir-fry for one minute. Add the mustard and the vinegar, then reduce by around half.

Add the octopus pieces, onion and capsicum and cook until all is tender.

To finish, season to taste with salt and pepper.

DEEP-FRIED FISH
WITH HOT & SOUR
LEMON GRASS SAUCE

INDONESIA

YIELD
4 servings
LEVEL OF DIFFICULTY
Easy
TIME
1 hour, 30 minutes

TAGS
Fry, gluten-free
CONTAINS
Chilli, fish, garlic, poultry

Reef fishermen mostly aim to catch snappers [Lutjanidae] and groupers [Serranidae], but there are other delicious fish down there – such as the hogfish [Lachnolaimus maximus] and triggerfish [Balistida]. All make a great choice for this recipe.

CHEF'S NOTE
If you do not like to deep-fry, just steam the fish. Any snapper variety can be used.

Palm sugar is considered a whole sugar and adds a rich flavour to any dish. It dissolves like regular sugar and contains vitamins, minerals and phytonutrients. You can find palm sugar in a health, Asian, Indian or Latin speciality food stores.

SERVE WITH
Steamed rice

FISH
4 fish fillets each **120 grams** (4 oz), with skin on
1 lemon, juiced
Pinch of **turmeric powder**
Pinch of **coriander powder**
Pinch chilli powder
Pinch of **salt**
Oil for **deep-frying**

SAUCE
2 tablespoons cooking oil
25 grams (1 tablespoon) **shallots,** chopped
50 grams (½ cup) **lemon grass,** finely chopped
25 grams (1 tablespoon) **garlic,** finely chopped
10 grams (2 tablespoons) **ginger,** grated
10 grams (2 teaspoons) chopped **red chilli** (depends on desired degree of spiciness)
30 grams (1½ tablespoons) **tomato,** chopped
25 ml (2 tablespoons) **chicken stock**
25 ml (2 tablespoons) **rice vinegar**
25 ml (2 tablespoons) **lime juice**
10 ml (1 tablespoon) **fish sauce**
15 grams (2 teaspoons) **tamarind paste**
25 grams (2 tablespoons) **palm sugar,** chopped, **to taste**

TO FINISH
Coriander (cilantro), roughly chopped

PREPARATION
Mix the fish in a bowl with the lemon juice, turmeric, coriander, chilli powder and salt. Cover and marinate in the refrigerator for one hour. Drain the fish well.

Heat the oil in a saucepan or fryer and deep-fry the fish until cooked and crispy. The oil needs to be hot, so it becomes crispy on the outside without overcooking the fish. Let the fillet rest on kitchen paper in order to absorb the oil.

For the sauce, heat the oil in a saucepan and sweat off the shallots and lemon grass.

Add the garlic, ginger and red chilli and stir-fry for another minute. Add the tomato and stir-fry for a few minutes.

Add all the remaining sauce ingredients and bring to a boil. Turn down the heat and cook until it has a thick sauce like consistency and fine-tune the seasoning.

To finish, place the fish fillets on the plates and spoon the hot and sour sauce over them.

Garnish with the coriander.

COCOCHURRI
CRUSTED FISH
AUSTRALIA

YIELD	TAGS
4 servings	Bake, gluten-free
LEVEL OF DIFFICULTY	CONTAINS
Easy	Chilli, coconut, dairy, egg,
TIME	fish, garlic
1 hour	

The profound flavours of this recipe are enhanced by "chimichurri sauce", which was brought to Australia by Spanish sailors.

In combination with grated coconut, the popular sauce becomes "cocochurri", which is perfect for baking fish.

CHEF'S NOTE
The cooking temperature depends on the thickness of the fish fillet. I use black-tip grouper (Vielle rouge) fillets, which are approximately 3 to 4 cm (1–1.5 in) thick. If you have a thicker fillet, reduce the heat slightly.

SERVE WITH
Coconut & sesame bread (see page 145)

INGREDIENTS
4 portions thick white fish fillet
each **120 grams** (4 oz), for example
sea bass or black cod, skinless
Salt and **white pepper to taste**

COCOCHURRI CRUST
2 tablespoons sherry vinegar
3 tablespoons lemon juice
3 tablespoons chopped **flat parsley**
2 tablespoons chopped **fresh oregano**
2 tablespoons chopped **garlic**
50 grams (⅓ cup)
green capsicum (bell pepper), chopped
50 grams (½ cup) **unsalted butter,** soft
1 egg yolk
50 grams (½ cup) **grated coconut**
Salt and **black pepper to taste**
Chilli flakes to taste

TO FINISH
1 lemon, sliced
1 garlic, halved

PREPARATION
First make the crust, which needs to cool before baking. To do so, combine all the crust ingredients in a food processor until it becomes a smooth paste. Season with the salt, pepper and chilli flakes to your taste. With a spatula spread the crust in a 0.5 cm (0.2 in) thick layer on a flat plate covered with baking paper. Refrigerate the crust so that it sets.

Heat the oven to 220° Celsius (425°F).

Season the fish with salt and pepper and place on an oiled baking tray. Add the lemon slices and garlic to the tray.

Remove the crust from the fridge and cut into same-size pieces as the fish fillets.

Place a piece of the crust on each fillet and bake until the fish is just done.

Make sure not to overcook the fish. Remove from the oven and serve.

LAKSA
COCONUT SOUP
INDONESIA

YIELD		**TAGS**
4 servings		Make ahead, soup
LEVEL OF DIFFICULTY		**CONTAINS**
Easy		Chilli, egg, garlic, seafood, soy, wheat
TIME		
1 hour, 30 minutes		

Laksa is a popular hot and sour coconut soup with origins in China and Malaysia. Laksa can be cooked with chicken, fish or seafood – as you like.

CHEF'S NOTE
To improve the flavour, you can add a few chicken bones while preparing the soup. Use water and prawn shells if shrimp stock is not available.

SERVE WITH
Egg or rice noodles

INGREDIENTS
3 tablespoons cooking oil
50 grams (⅓ cup) **red onion,** chopped
2 tablespoons chopped **garlic**
3 tablespoons chopped **ginger**
50 grams (½ cup) **lemon grass,** chopped, the white part only
2 tablespoons sliced & seeded **red chilli**
2 tablespoons turmeric powder
1 teaspoon coriander powder
1 teaspoon cumin powder
20 grams (1 tablespoon) **shrimp paste**
20 grams (2 teaspoons) **tamarind paste**
600 ml (2½ cups) **coconut milk**
400 ml (1⅔ cups) **shrimp stock**
20 grams (1 cup) **Fresh kaffir lime leaves**
Fish sauce and **lime juice to taste**

TO FINISH
100 grams (1 cup) **prawns** (shrimp), cleaned, peeled and deveined
50 grams (1 cup) **button mushrooms,** sliced
50 grams (⅓ cup) **carrot,** julienned
100 grams (1 cup) **bok choy,** torn apart
50 grams (⅓ cup) **cherry tomatoes,** halved
1 egg, boiled and quartered
50 grams (½ cup) **soybean sprouts**
Fresh coriander (cilantro), thinly sliced

PREPARATION
Heat the oil in a heavy soup pot and sweat off the onion, garlic and ginger.

Add the chopped lemon grass, chilli, turmeric, coriander and cumin powder and fry gently for five minutes.

Add the shrimp paste and the tamarind paste. Fry for a few seconds, then add the coconut milk, shrimp stock and kaffir lime leaves and simmer for about 20 minutes.

Strain through a sieve and adjust seasoning with the fish sauce and lime juice.

To finish, bring the soup back to a boil, add first the prawns and cook for one minute, then add the mushrooms, carrots, bok choy and tomatoes.

Cook until all is just tender.

Garnish the soup with the egg, soybean sprouts and some fresh coriander.

SOFT-SHELL CRAB
PAKORA

SRI LANKA

YIELD
4 servings

LEVEL OF DIFFICULTY
Medium

TIME
1 hour

TAGS
Fry, gluten-free

CONTAINS
Chilli, seafood

The soft-shell crab is a common marine crab also known as shore crab. The crabs are sorted and selected just before the (soft) shell starts to solidify, which means that almost the entire crab can be eaten.

The crabs are still harvested with traditional methods, which are deeply rooted within the fishermen's families.

CHEF'S NOTE

When buying soft-shell crabs, live ones are the best (not easy to find). To select the tastiest, use your nose. They should smell clean and astringent, like sea mist.

To clean soft-shell crabs, cut off the front of the crab, about 2 cm (0.75 in) behind the eye and mouth. Squeeze out the contents of the sack which is just behind the cuts you just made. Remove and discard the gills. Rinse the entire crab well and pat dry.

PAKORA BATTER

120 grams (1 cup) **chickpea flour** (also called gram flour or besan)
1 teaspoon cumin powder
1 teaspoon coriander powder
1 teaspoon turmeric powder
1 teaspoon coriander seeds, ground
120 ml (½ cup) **sparkling soda water**
Salt and **pepper to taste**

CORIANDER MINT CHUTNEY

30 grams (1½ cups) **coriander** (cilantro) **leaves**
30 grams (1 cup) **mint leaves**
30 grams (2 tablespoons) **red onion,** roughly sliced
2 tablespoons lemon juice
1 green chilli
1 tablespoon water
Pinch of **salt**
Pinch of **sugar**

TO FINISH

600 grams (1.3 oz) **soft-shell crabs**
Oil for deep-frying
Pinch of **"chaat masala"** (see page 109)
2 limes, halved
Sea salt to taste

PREPARATION

To make the batter, whisk all the batter ingredients in a bowl and let the mixture rest for 30 minutes. The consistency should be a bit thicker than a crepe batter.

For the coriander mint chutney, mix all the ingredients in a food processor and set aside until ready to serve.

To finish, heat the oil in a saucepan or a fryer to 180° Celsius (320°F). Coat the dry soft-shell crabs with the pakora batter and deep-fry until cooked and crispy. Make sure not to move the crabs too much while frying so the batter does not fall off.

When cooked, let the fried crabs rest on kitchen paper, and while still hot, season with a pinch of **"chaat masala"** (see page 109), sea salt and serve with the lime halves and coriander mint chutney.

STEAMED FISH
WITH GARLIC-LIME
& CHILLI BROTH
INDONESIA

YIELD
4 servings
LEVEL OF DIFFICULTY
Easy
TIME
30 minutes

TAGS
Gluten-free, soup
CONTAINS
Chilli, fish, garlic

This is an incredibly popular dish with Thai heritage. While in Asia fish is usually steamed whole, we prefer to fillet it. This not only makes it easier to steam, there are also no bones to deal with.

A great way to eat healthily without sacrificing taste.

CHEF'S NOTE
The best way to make this dish is to add the sauce after the fish has been steamed (steaming the sauce will make the lime juice bitter). As always use as few or as many chillies as you can handle.

SERVE WITH
Rice

INGREDIENTS
4 sea bass fillet each 120 grams (4 oz), with the skin on

BROTH
40 grams (2½ tablespoons) **garlic,** finely chopped
20 grams (4 tablespoons) **chillies,** sliced (or to your liking)
40 ml (2½ tablespoons) **fish stock** (or water)
40 ml (2½ tablespoons) **lime juice**
3 tablespoons fish sauce
30 ml (2 tablespoons) **mild, liquid honey**

TO FINISH
Scallions, sliced
Coriander (cilantro) **leaves**
Lime slices
Salt to taste

PREPARATION
Steam the fish in a bamboo basket or steamer until cooked and arrange on deep plates.

Make the broth while steaming the fish by simmering all the broth ingredients in a saucepan for a few minutes.

To serve, pour the broth over the fish fillets. Garnish with the scallions, coriander leaves and lime.

Season to taste and serve.

SALADE D'OURSINS
SEA URCHIN SALAD

MAURITIUS

YIELD
4 servings
LEVEL OF DIFFICULTY
Easy
TIME
45 minutes

TAGS
Raw
CONTAINS
Chilli, fish, seafood

Those of you who surf know how unpleasant sea urchins can be, but you might be surprised to learn that they can be more than just a nasty sting in your foot.

We just dive and harvest them using our hands. We have never been injured so far, perhaps due to practice or just pure luck or the fact that we wear gloves. Sometimes we crack them open on the boat and simply spread the insides on bread and enjoy with a squeeze of lime.

CHEF'S NOTE
In Japan, sea urchins (uni) are often eaten as sashimi or sushi. With its unique sweet flavour, the roe is also delicious to use with pasta, in sauces or soups.

SERVE WITH
Toasted bread

INGREDIENTS
12 sea urchins

SALAD
50 grams (⅓ cup) **cucumber,** thinly sliced
1 small red onion, thinly sliced
1 tablespoon finely chopped **red chilli**
20 ml (1 tablespoon) **lime juice**
20 ml (1 tablespoon) **fish sauce**
20 ml (1 tablespoon) **liquid honey**
1 tablespoon chopped **coriander** (cilantro)
Season to taste

PREPARATION
Place the sea urchins on a chopping board with their mouths up (upside down). Using scissors cut a circle around the mouths big enough to use it as a small serving bowl.

Drain and remove the liquid and the dark coloured organs from the shell. With a spoon remove the orange roe and set aside to make the salad.

Do not keep the roe for long; try to serve it as soon as possible. Rinse each shell with cold water and be sure not to leave any loose shell parts.

Set the shells aside to use as salad bowls.

Combine all the ingredients for the salad, and at the end gently add the sea urchin roe.

Season to taste with salt, then spoon the salad back into the shells just before serving.

MEAT & POULTRY

'NOT EATING MEAT IS A DECISION, EATING MEAT IS AN INSTINCT'

~ Denis Leary ~

AKOHO SY VOANIO
CHICKEN CURRY WITH
COCONUT AND LEMON
COMOROS

YIELD
4 servings
LEVEL OF DIFFICULTY
Easy, but slow
TIME
4 hours in total

TAGS
Slow cooking
CONTAINS
Chilli, coconut, dairy, garlic, poultry

"Akoho sy Voanio" – originally, a Malagasy dish – is among the most popular dishes in Comoros and Madagascar, especially around Christmas time.

This version is my favourite and tastes great all year. The green capsicum (also known as peppers), sweet paprika and Tabasco®, lend a fantastic round flavour to this stew.

CHEF'S NOTE
If the tomato is not sweet enough, add a little honey or brown sugar. This stew needs a sweet, sour and spicy note.

SERVE WITH
Steamed rice

CHICKEN
600 grams (1.3 lb)
boneless chicken thighs
1 tablespoon turmeric powder
1 teaspoon coriander powder
1 teaspoon cumin powder
2 tablespoons lemon juice
1 tablespoon lemon zest
1 teaspoon chilli powder

STEW
50 ml (¼ cup) **coconut oil,** divided
100 grams (½ cup) **onion,** sliced
100 grams (¾ cup)
green capsicum (bell pepper), sliced
15 grams (1 tablespoon) **garlic,** chopped
15 grams (2 tablespoons) **ginger,** chopped
100 grams (⅔ cup) **tomato,**
roughly chopped
1 tablespoon turmeric powder
1 teaspoon coriander powder
1 teaspoon cumin powder
2 tablespoons sweet paprika powder
1 teaspoon chilli powder
50 ml (¼ cup) **lemon juice**
200 ml (¾ cup plus 2 tablespoons)
chicken stock
3 bay leaves
200 ml (¾ cup) **coconut cream**

TO FINISH
Green Tabasco® to taste
Salt & black pepper to taste
Crème fraîche
Lemon zest
Coriander (cilantro), chopped
Fried **chillies**

PREPARATION
First marinate the chicken with all ingredients. Use a sufficiently large bowl and your hands for even distribution. Cover the bowl and let marinate in the refrigerator for at least two hours.

Heat a saucepan with a spoonful of the coconut oil and fry the chicken over medium to high heat until it is nicely browned. Remove the chicken from the saucepan and set aside.

To make the stew, lower the heat slightly and gently sweat the onions in the rest of the coconut oil until soft.

Add the capsicum, garlic, ginger and tomato and keep frying gently until all ingredients are soft. Add the turmeric, coriander and cumin powder, then gently stir-fry for about five minutes.

Add the sweet paprika and chilli powder, stir-fry for about 30 seconds and quickly add the lemon juice and chicken stock, taking care that the sweet paprika does not turn bitter. Add the bay leaves and slowly simmer the stew covered with a lid for about one hour to infuse all flavours.

Return the chicken to the stew, add the coconut cream and cook until the chicken is done and the stew has a nice creamy consistency.

To finish, season the stew with the green Tabasco, salt and pepper. Garnish the plates with a dollop of the crème fraîche, lemon zest, coriander and chillies.

DUCK SALMI
MAURITIUS

YIELD
4 servings
LEVEL OF DIFFICULTY
Easy
TIME
1 hour, marinate for 8 hours

CONTAINS
Chilli, garlic, meat, soy, wheat

Salmi originates from traditional French cuisine and has been widely adopted – and adapted – in Mauritian households.

The Mauritian version is a semi-dry curry dish that is traditionally eaten in the cooler season because of its warmth and very strong spices.

Salmi is most popular with duck, chicken or venison. The marinade is what makes it special for the holidays.

CHEF'S NOTE
The recipe features very powerful cinnamon and clove flavours. That is how the locals eat it. Simply reduce the amount of salmi paste for a lighter version.

SERVE WITH
Steamed rice

INGREDIENTS

4 duck legs, with skin and bones
100 ml (½ cup) **red wine,** divided
1 tablespoon salt
3 tablespoons dark soy sauce
3 tablespoons salmi paste (see page 111)
2 tablespoons cooking oil
120 grams (¾ cup) **red onion,** chopped
50 grams (6 tablespoons) **garlic,** chopped
150 grams (¾ cup) **tomato,** diced
2 sprigs thyme
2 tablespoons brown sugar
200 ml (¾ cup) **water**

TO FINISH
Coriander (cilantro) leaves

PREPARATION
First marinate the duck legs. Combine half the red wine, salt and soy with the **salmi paste** (see page 111) in a small bowl. Rub the mixture onto the duck legs. Cover and keep refrigerated for at least eight hours.

Heat a casserole pan with the oil over medium to high heat. Remove the duck legs from their marinade and pat them dry with a paper towel. Discard the marinade liquid. Fry the duck legs until nicely browned on all sides. The duck legs need not be cooked all the way through. Remove the duck legs and set aside.

Lower the heat to medium. Add the onion and garlic to the casserole pan and sweat off. Add the tomato, thyme and brown sugar. Deglaze the pan with the remaining red wine.

Return the duck legs to the casserole. Add the water, cover with a lid and cook gently over low heat until the duck legs are ready. If necessary, add some water during the cooking process.

To finish, garnish the dish with the coriander.

PITIPOA SY HENAKISOA
PORK & PEA STEW
MADAGASCAR

YIELD
4 servings
LEVEL OF DIFFICULTY
Easy
TIME
1 hour, 50 minutes

TAGS
Gluten-free, stew
CONTAINS
Garlic, pork

Traditional Malagasy food includes plenty of meat stews with seasoning that is quite bland. I therefore made it a bit more exciting with paprika powder and cayenne pepper, which are not in the original recipe. I also use salted pork knuckle instead of minced pork to lend extra flavour.

SERVE WITH
Steamed rice

INGREDIENTS

5 tablespoons **cooking oil**
1.5 kilograms (3.3 lb) **salted pork knuckle,** sliced like "osso bucco"
70 grams (½ cup) **onion,** chopped
30 grams (2 tablespoons) **garlic,** chopped
50 ml (3 tablespoons) **white vinegar**
200 grams (1 cup) **tomato,** chopped
1 tablespoon **paprika powder**
1 teaspoon **cayenne pepper**
500 ml (2 cups) **chicken or pork stock**
5 **bay leaves**

TO FINISH

200 grams (1½ cup) **green peas,** cooked
Season to taste

PREPARATION

Heat a casserole pan with the oil over high heat and sear the pork knuckles until they are golden brown in colour. Remove the pork and set aside.

Lower the heat slightly and add the onion and garlic to the casserole pan, sweat off and deglaze with the vinegar.

Add the tomato, paprika powder and cayenne pepper and cook for another minute.

Add the stock and bay leaves and return the pork knuckle to the pan. Cover the pan with a lid and simmer gently for approximately 1½ hours until tender.

To finish, add the green peas and season with salt.

CHILLI BEEF
INDONESIA

YIELD
4 servings
LEVEL OF DIFFICULTY
Easy
TIME
45 minutes

TAGS
Gluten-free
CONTAINS
Chilli, fish, garlic, meat

The majority of Indonesia's population are observant Muslims. This has naturally impacted their traditional diet and beef is used in many of these dishes.

Here is one very popular beef recipe that I brought back from Indonesia.

CHEF'S NOTE
Keep the chilli sauce in an airtight container in the fridge and use it for another meal.

SERVE WITH
Steamed rice

CHILLI SAUCE
3 tablespoons cooking oil
120 grams (½ cup)
red onion, finely chopped
60 grams (5 tablespoons)
garlic, finely chopped
60 grams (6 tablespoons)
ginger, finely chopped
4 tablespoons dry red chilli flakes
50 ml (3½ tablespoons) **tomato ketchup**
50 ml (3½ tablespoons) **mild liquid honey**
100 ml (7 tablespoons) **water**
5 tablespoons Worcestershire sauce
100 ml (7 tablespoons) **oyster sauce**
1 tablespoon sesame oil

MEAT
3 tablespoons cooking oil
600 grams (1.3 lb) **beef tenderloin,**
cut into 5 cm (2 in) cubes at
room temperature
10 dried chillies, soaked in
water for 10 minutes
100 grams (1 medium) **red onion,** cut into
quarters and broken up into its layers
100 ml (7 tablespoons) **chilli sauce**

TO FINISH
Salt and **pepper to taste**
Spring onion, thinly sliced

PREPARATION
To make the chilli sauce, heat the oil in a saucepan over medium heat. Sweat off the onions, garlic and ginger. Add the chilli flakes, stir-fry for one minute, then add the ketchup, honey, water, Worcestershire sauce and oyster sauce. Bring to a boil, then lower the heat and simmer for about 15 minutes until all the flavours are infused. Finish the sauce with sesame oil. This makes about 500 ml (2 cups) of chilli sauce.

Season the beef cubes with salt and pepper.

Heat a wok with the oil and sauté the beef until nicely browned.

Add the chillies and onion, stir-fry for one minute. The onion should still have a bit of a crunch.

Add the chilli sauce and cook until the beef is done to your liking.

To finish, arrange the chilli beef in a bowl, season with salt and pepper and garnish with the spring onions.

RO-PATSA
BEEF & POTATO STEW
WITH DRIED SHRIMPS
MADAGASCAR

YIELD
4 servings
LEVEL OF DIFFICULTY
Easy
TIME
3 hours

TAGS
Gluten-free, make ahead, slow cooking, stew, one-pot meal
CONTAINS
Chilli, seafood, meat

This Malagasy beef and potato stew reputedly restores health, is a popular home remedy for any ill, and is also believed to benefit nursing mothers.

To improve the taste in my version, I use the original recipe, but use whole beef short ribs instead of diced beef.

SERVE WITH
Baguette

INGREDIENTS

5 tablespoons cooking oil
800 grams (1.7 lb) **beef short ribs,** cut between the ribs, at room temperature
150 grams (⅔ cup) **onion,** chopped
100 grams (½ cup) **tomato,** diced
3 red chillies, sliced
300 ml (1¼ cups) **beef stock**
2 tablespoons dried shrimps
5 bay leaves
Season to taste

TO FINISH

300 grams (1½ cups) **potatoes,** cut into small cubes
Salt to taste
Parsley, chopped

PREPARATION

Heat a stock pot with the oil untill it reaches the smoking point. Sear the ribs until brown in colour on all sides. Remove the meat and set aside.

Add the onion to the pot and fry until it is also turns golden brown.

Add the tomato and red chilli and stir-fry for another minute.

Return the beef ribs to the stock pot, add the stock, dried shrimp and bay leaves, season with salt and cook covered over low heat for approximately two hours.

Add some more stock if needed while cooking.

When the meat almost falls off the bone remove from the sauce and set aside.

To finish, add the potato cubes to the sauce and cook until tender.

Return the ribs to the sauce. Let the meat gently reheat and adjust the final seasoning if required.

Garnish the dish with the parsley.

CABRI MASALA

RÉUNION

YIELD
4 servings

LEVEL OF DIFFICULTY
Easy

TIME
1 hour

TAGS
Gluten-free, make ahead, stew

CONTAINS
Chilli, garlic, meat

I am not familiar with the origin of this dish, but in most simple Creole dinners, you will find chicken curry (the locals call it cari) fish curry, wild duck, and even curried tenrec (a type of hedgehog).

In Réunion, the curries are not generally made with as much fiery heat as in other curry nations, but with the basic ingredients of onion, turmeric, chilli and garlic. Masale, or garam masala – the spice used in every home on the island – binds the curry with its finishing flourish.

CHEF'S NOTE
The original recipe is quite dry. It is up to you whether you prefer to make it that way. If not, simply add more water. Adding tomatoes when combining the spices gives the dish a more balanced taste. If you cannot find curry leaves – just omit them.

SERVE WITH
Steamed rice or "mkatra foutra" (see page 145)

INGREDIENTS
5 tablespoons cooking oil
500 grams (1.1 oz) **goat meat,** cut into 3 cm (1.2 in) cubes at room temperature
200 grams (⅔ cup) **onion,** chopped
30 grams (2 tablespoons) **garlic,** chopped
1 teaspoon cumin powder
1 tablespoon curry powder
1 teaspoon chilli powder
7 curry leaves

TO FINISH
Salt to taste

PREPARATION
Heat the oil over medium to high heat in a curry pot (or saucepan) until it smokes.

Add the goat meat and cook until brown, remove and set aside.

Add the onion and garlic and sauté until they turn golden brown.

Add the cumin, curry, chilli powder and curry leaves. Stir-fry for three minutes and return the meat to the pot.

Add water until the meat is covered.

Cover the pan with a lid and cook over low heat until the meat is tender.

To finish, season with salt.

LAMB SHANK
IN ONION GRAVY
MADAGASCAR

YIELD
4 servings
LEVEL OF DIFFICULTY
Easy
TIME
2 hours, 30 minutes

TAGS
Bake, make ahead, slow cooking
CONTAINS
Chilli, garlic, meat, soy, wheat

Congenial tasty treats from Indonesia, India, the Middle East, China and Europe influenced this recipe and made it the most cosmopolitan approach to a traditional Malagasy dish.

CHEF'S NOTE
You can substitute tomato paste for fresh tomato and vegetable stock for lamb stock if not available.

Palm sugar is considered a whole sugar and adds a rich flavour to any dish; it dissolves like regular sugar and contains vitamins, minerals and phytonutrients. You can find palm sugar in health food, Asian, Indian or Latin speciality food stores.

SERVE WITH
Steamed rice

INGREDIENTS
4 (or 8 small) lamb shanks, at room temperature
2 tablespoons cooking oil
4 large onions, thinly sliced
4 cloves garlic, chopped
2 tablespoons ginger paste
2 pieces lemon grass, chopped
2 red chillies, seeds removed and finely chopped
4 tomatoes, roughly chopped
1 tablespoon brown sugar
25 ml (5 teaspoons) **lime juice**
500 ml (2 cups) **lamb stock**
4 whole star anise
20 grams (¾ cup) stalk of **Thai basil**
20 grams (¾ cup) stalk of **mint**
20 grams (¾ cup) stalk of **coriander** (cilantro)
25 ml (1½ tablespoons) **soy sauce**

TO FINISH
Salt and **pepper to taste**
2 tablespoons palm sugar (or mild honey)
Mint, finely chopped

PREPARATION
Heat the oil in a casserole pot over medium to high heat, then brown the lamb shanks on all sides. Remove the shanks and set aside.

Add the onions, ginger, garlic, lemon grass and chilli and fry until soft. Add the tomatoes and sugar and stir-fry for another 5 minutes. Add all the remaining ingredients and bring to a boil.

Heat the oven to 120° Celsius (250°F).

Return the lamb shanks to the casserole pot, cover with a lid and place in the preheated oven. Cook for about 1 hour and 30 minutes until the lamb is soft and tender. Remove the lamb shanks from the gravy and set aside. Remove the herb stalks. Reduce the stock on medium heat until it reaches a thick onion gravy-like consistency.

To finish, adjust seasoning with salt, pepper and add the palm sugar. Return the shanks to the gravy. Cook until the shanks are hot and the sugar is dissolved, sprinkle with mint.

LASOPY SINOA
MADAGASCAR

YIELD
4 servings
LEVEL OF DIFFICULTY
Easy
TIME
30 minutes

TAGS
One-pot meal, soup
CONTAINS
Chilli, egg, garlic, poultry,
sesame, soy, wheat

"Lasopy Sinoa" (soupe chinoise) is primarily influenced by Austronesian cuisine, but as with every local speciality over time, the recipe has been adapted to the many tastes of the refugees, traders, explorers, wayfarers and settlers who came to this colourful island.

CHEF'S NOTE
You can use water instead of stock as the minced meat provides plenty of flavour.

INGREDIENTS
3 tablespoons **cooking oil**
200 grams (7 oz) **minced chicken**
3 tablespoons chopped **onion**
1 tablespoon chopped **garlic**
1 tablespoon chopped **ginger**
1 litre (4 cups) **chicken stock**
3 tablespoons **soy sauce**
1 **red chilli**, sliced
200 grams (7 oz) **fresh egg noodles**
Salt and **black pepper to taste**

TO FINISH
2 **eggs**, beaten
Salt and **black pepper to taste**
4 tablespoons thinly sliced **spring onion**
2 tablespoons chopped **coriander** (cilantro)
A few drops of **sesame oil**

PREPARATION
Heat the oil in a soup pot over medium heat. Fry the minced meat, then add the onion, garlic and ginger and gently stir-fry for a few minutes, making sure that they do not brown in colour. Add the stock and bring to a boil, removing any froth that forms on the surface.

Add the soy sauce and the sliced red chilli. Add the noodles and cook until they are done. Season with salt and black pepper.

To finish, fry the eggs in a separate pan, season with salt and black pepper. Cut the fried eggs into thin slices.

Divide soup into portions and garnish with the sliced eggs, spring onion, coriander and sesame oil.

SLOW-COOKED PORK BELLY

INDONESIA

YIELD
4 servings

LEVEL OF DIFFICULTY
Medium

TIME
3 hours

TAGS
Fry, make ahead, slow cooking

CONTAINS
Chilli, garlic, pork

With the influence of hundreds of ethnic groups mixed with foreign notes, Indonesian cuisine is vibrant, colourful and full of flavour. While a large part of the country basically omits pork dishes – there are some which have been introduced through Chinese Malay immigrants.

CHEF'S NOTE
You can cook the pork belly in advance. Just before serving fry the pork and serve with its glaze.

PORK BELLY
1 litre (4 cups) **chicken stock** (or vegetable stock)
20 grams (2 tablespoons) **ginger,** chopped
20 grams (1½ tablespoons) **garlic,** chopped
2 tablespoons **rice vinegar**
2 tablespoons **white sugar**
Salt and **pepper** to taste
800 grams (1.7 lb) **pork belly**

GLAZE
2 tablespoons **cooking oil**
20 grams (1½ tablespoons) **onion,** finely chopped
20 grams (1½ tablespoons) **garlic,** finely chopped
20 grams (2 tablespoons) **ginger,** finely chopped
2 stalks **lemon grass,** finely chopped
20 grams (3 tablespoons) **red chilli,** chopped (or to taste)
30 ml (2 tablespoons) **soy sauce**
30 ml (2 tablespoons) **rice vinegar**
20 ml (1½ tablespoons) **liquid honey**
1 teaspoon **cornstarch**
3 tablespoons **water**
Salt to taste

TO FINISH
Oil for deep frying
Coriander (cilantro), chopped

PREPARATION
First cook the pork until tender. Place the stock, all pork belly ingredients and the pork belly in a pan and bring to a boil. Cover with a lid, lower the heat and let the pork belly simmer gently for approximately two hours until the pork is very tender. Insert a fork into the pork belly to check its softness.

When done, remove the pork belly carefully from the stock, let cool and keep refrigerated.

For the glaze, heat the oil in a saucepan. Sweat off the onion, garlic, ginger and lemon grass.

Add the chilli, soy sauce, rice vinegar and honey and bring to a slow boil.

Mix the cornstarch with the water in a small bowl, then whisk the mixture into the sauce and let thicken on low heat for at least 10 minutes. Season to taste. Let the glaze cool.

To finish, cut the pork belly into cubes and deep-fry in hot oil until crispy. Remove it from the oil and let rest on kitchen paper.

In a saucepan reheat some of the glaze, add the crispy pork, and mix gently until the pork is well coated.

Arrange on a plate and garnish with the coriander.

HALIM
LAMB SOUP WITH
LENTILS & BARLEY

MAURITIUS

YIELD
4 servings

LEVEL OF DIFFICULTY
Easy

TIME
1 hour, 30 minutes

TAGS
One-pot meal, soup

CONTAINS
Chilli, garlic, meat, soy, wheat

"Halim" (haleem) is a popular Arabian dish which, at some point, was adopted by the Indians. The Hindu community of Mauritius introduced halim to the islanders, who embraced and adapted the recipe.

This is the Mauritian way to prepare a proper halim. Enjoy!

CHEF'S NOTE
Adjust the consistency with water if the soup is too thick, and if the soup is too liquid, add some rolled oats. The ground barley can be substituted for bulgur or ground wheat.

INGREDIENTS
4 tablespoons cooking oil
100 grams (3.5 oz) lamb, cut into cubes (½ cm, 0.2 in), at room temperature
1 large white onion, chopped
5 cloves garlic, chopped
1 tablespoon chopped ginger
1 teaspoon turmeric powder
1 teaspoon chilli powder
1 tablespoon cumin powder
1 teaspoon cinnamon powder
1 teaspoon cardamom powder
1 teaspoon ground black pepper
500 ml (2 cups) water
100 grams (6 tablespoons) yellow and black lentils, mixed
60 grams (2 oz) ground barley
Pinch of salt

TO FINISH
Coriander (cilantro), freshly chopped
Salt to taste
Lemon juice to taste

PREPARATION
Heat the oil in a casserole pan and sauté the meat with the onion, garlic and ginger.

Add the dry spices and sauté for another 10 minutes to release the aroma.

Add the water, lentils, ground barley and salt. Cook until the meat, barley and lentils are tender.

To finish, add the coriander and season to taste with salt and lemon juice.

CHICKEN & COCONUT SOUP WITH GALANGAL

INDONESIA

YIELD
4 servings

LEVEL OF DIFFICULTY
Easy

TIME
1 hour, 30 minutes

TAGS
One-pot meal, soup, slow cooking

CONTAINS
Chilli, chicken, coconut, soy, wheat

"Galangal" [Zingiberacea] is a plant in the ginger family that is mainly used in Vietnamese and Indonesian cuisine. While galangal is from the same plant family, the taste is very different.

This is one of my favourite soup recipes. It is so simple to prepare, yet amazingly balanced in flavour.

CHEF'S NOTE
If you prefer a spicy soup, add more red chillies at the beginning of the cooking process. The soup also makes a good base for a seafood soup or even a vegetarian soup, just omit or substitute the chicken.

Galangal is very hard and requires a sharp knife.

INGREDIENTS
2 tablespoons cooking oil
50 grams (⅓ cup) **white onion**, sliced
50 grams (⅓ cup) **galangal,** sliced
½ chicken
15 grams (½ cup) **coriander stems** (cilantro), with leaves on
1 tablespoon black whole peppercorns
3 stalks **lemon grass,** cut in half
15 grams (⅔ cup) **kaffir lime leaves**
1 litre (4 cups) **water**
200 ml (¾ cup plus 2 tablespoons) **coconut cream**
15 ml (1 tablespoon) **soy sauce**
50 ml (3½ tablespoons) **lime juice**

TO FINISH
Red chilli, sliced
Coriander (cilantro), roughly chopped

PREPARATION
Heat the oil over medium heat in a soup pot. Sweat off the onion and galangal.

Add the chicken, water and all the remaining ingredients. Simmer gently for one hour.

Remove the chicken, let it cool slightly and use your fingers to remove the meat from the bones, pull the meat into bite-size pieces and set aside.

Strain the soup through a fine sieve and season to taste.

To finish, divide the soup into portions, add pieces of chicken and garnish with the chilli and coriander.

SURF & TURF WITH WASABI BÉARNAISE

AUSTRALIA

YIELD
4 servings
LEVEL OF DIFFICULTY
Medium
TIME
1 hour

TAGS
Grill, gluten-free
CONTAINS
Chilli, dairy, seafood, meat

When talking about Australia's best food, surf & turf easily tops the list. The culture of BBQ is deeply rooted in the Commonwealth of Australia, and the people embrace every opportunity to grill their meats and seafood. But of course, no BBQ would be complete without a myriad of seasonings, rubs and sauces (and beer) and every family takes huge pride in their creations.

The wasabi Béarnaise, I created for this recipe combines beef and seafood in a way that I have never tasted before.

CHEF'S NOTE

To make clarified butter, melt butter in a small sauce pan on low heat. Let it simmer gently until the foam rises to the top of the melted butter. When no more foam seems to be rising to the surface, remove from the heat and skim it off with a spoon. Then strain the butter and keep liquid for use for the wasabi Béarnaise.

SERVE WITH

Damper bread (see page 165)

WASABI BÉARNAISE

100 ml (6½ tablespoons) **tarragon vinegar**
2 tablespoons chopped shallots
1 tablespoon whole black peppercorns
2 egg yolks
100 ml (6½ tablespoons) **clarified butter** (ghee), melted
2 tablespoons chopped **tarragon**
½ **lemon,** squeezed
Wasabi paste to taste
Salt to taste

TO FINISH

4 beef steaks, at room temperature
4 giant prawns (shrimps) in the shell, cut lengthwise into halves
BBQ seasoning (see page 107)
Oil to brush the steak and prawns
Sea salt to taste

PREPARATION

First make the wasabi Béarnaise. Boil the vinegar, shallots and peppercorns in a small saucepan and reduce to a quarter (25 ml, 1½ tablespoons). In the meantime, prepare a double boiler. Fill a pan with water, bring to a slow boil and nestle a mixing bowl above it. It is important that the water does not have direct contact with the mixing bowl.

Strain the vinegar reduction into the bowl of the double boiler. Whisk in the egg yolks and whisk continuously, never stopping. This process takes a couple of minutes. As soon as the mixture starts to thicken remove the bowl from the simmering water but keep on whisking to make a sabayon. You are now cooling down the sabayon. Return the sabayon to the double boiler and slowly drizzle in the butter while whisking continuously. If at any time the sauce looks as if it is about to separate, remove it from the double boiler and continue whisking to cool it down or whisk in one teaspoon of cold water. When all the butter is incorporated, remove the bowl from the heat and add the chopped tarragon, lemon juice and wasabi paste and salt to your taste.

Put aside until the BBQ is ready. If you want to cover the "Béarnaise" use plastic cling wrap. Cover without any air in between the sauce and the wrap to keep the sauce from changing colour.

To finish, rub the steaks with a pinch of the **BBQ seasoning** (see page 107), brush with oil and grill on a BBQ to your liking.

Grill the meat first, then let it rest covered with aluminium foil for a few minutes before serving. Meanwhile, season the prawns with the BBQ seasoning, brush with the oil and grill. Serve the steaks and prawns together with the wasabi Béarnaise and sprinkle with sea salt to taste.

SPICES

'EVEN JUST A FEW SPICES
CAN TURN YOUR MUNDANE
DISHES INTO A CULINARY
MASTERPIECE'

~ Marcus Samuelson ~

GREEN
CURRY PASTE

MALDIVES

YIELD
1 cup
LEVEL OF DIFFICULTY
Easy
TIME
20 minutes

TAGS
Make ahead
CONTAINS
Chilli, coconut, mustard

The traditional green curry originates in Thailand and has become widely popular in the Asian and Indian cuisines. If you think that this is the mild curry, you are mistaken.

Customary "Maldives Curry" is prepared with freshly grated coconut, lime juice and cassava leaves.

While there are thousands of excellent variations of green curry, and every family would swear that theirs is the only one, I have developed my own recipe which, naturally, I like best.

USE FOR
"Mas riha" (see page 47)
Fish curry

INGREDIENTS

100 grams (1 cup) **coconut flakes**
1 tablespoon fennel seeds
1 tablespoon cloves
100 ml (½ cup) **lime juice**
30 grams (2 tablespoons) **chilli**
50 grams (3 tablespoons) **cassava leaves**
1 tablespoon turmeric powder
1 teaspoon mustard seeds
Coconut oil, if required

PREPARATION

Roast the coconut flakes, fennel seeds and cloves without oil in a frying pan (stirring often) or in the oven at 180° Celsius (355°F) until they start to brown and become fragrant. Let them cool off.

Combine all the ingredients and grind with a mortar and pestle until the ingredients become a paste.

If the paste is too dry, add some coconut oil.

Alternatively, you can use a food processor.

Store the paste in an airtight container.

You can keep the paste refrigerated for at least six months.

BBQ SEASONING
AUSTRALIA

YIELD
1 cup
LEVEL OF DIFFICULTY
Easy
TIME
20 minutes

TAGS
Make ahead
CONTAINS
Chilli, coconut, mustard

Every Australian BBQ lover will agree with me: no proper grill should go without a great seasoning. Since the Aussies know pretty much everything there is to know about grilling, I took their best recipe as my personal benchmark.

Sweet and smoky with a hint of spices, well-trimmed and perfect for indoor and outdoor grilling, roasting, and slow cooking.

USE FOR
As BBQ seasoning for fish, seafood, meat or vegetables

INGREDIENTS
20 grams (3 tablespoons) **onion granulate**
20 grams (2 tablespoons) **garlic powder**
10 grams (2 tablespoons) **cayenne pepper**
10 grams (4 teaspoons) **black whole peppercorns**
5 grams (4 teaspoons) **ginger powder**
20 grams (3 tablespoons) **mustard seed powder**
10 grams (2 teaspoons) **celery salt**
40 grams (3 tablespoons) **rock salt**
5 lemons, zested
10 thyme sprigs, leaves only

PREPARATION
Grind all the ingredients with a mortar and a pestle.

Alternatively you can use a food processor.

Store in the refrigerator in an airtight container.

CHAAT MASALA

SRI LANKA

YIELD	TAGS
4 servings	Make ahead
LEVEL OF DIFFICULTY	
Easy	
TIME	
30 minutes	

Traditional "chaat masala" is a slightly hot, somewhat sour, spice powder mix with roots in the Indian, Bangladeshi and Sri Lankan cuisine.

The mix travelled with traders and explorers across the Indian Ocean and found its way into traditional Aquacasian cuisine.

The unique taste of "chaat" comes from the black salt. It can be used to season all kinds of food.

USE FOR
Soft-shell crab pakora (see page 63)
Beef patties (see page 147)

INGREDIENTS
4 tablespoons coriander seeds
2 tablespoons cumin seeds
1 tablespoon carom seeds (ajwain)
2 tablespoons salt
1 tablespoon black salt
1½ tablespoons dry mango powder
2 tablespoons black peppercorns

PREPARATION
In a small frying pan, roast the coriander seeds, cumin seeds and the carom seeds – each separately – over low heat for a few minutes until they start to become aromatic. It is important that you roast each spice separately, because each requires a different roast time. Let all the spices cool.

Combine all ingredients and grind them into a fine powder either with a mortar and pestle or alternatively you can use a food processor.

Store in an airtight container.

110

SALMI PASTE

MAURITIUS

YIELD
¼ cup
LEVEL OF DIFFICULTY
Easy
TIME
20 minutes

TAGS
Make ahead
CONTAINS
Chilli, garlic

While "salmi" originated in France, as you have surely realised by now, nothing that made its way to the islands of the Indian Ocean has remained untouched.

The classic salmi sauce has been adapted, changed and upgraded over generations and the result is a salmi paste that is far better than the original.

Salmi spices are ideal for marinating poultry and game. They are very strong in flavour and mostly used in cooler seasons.

CHEF'S NOTE
On the islands they use a "ross cari" to crush the spices, which is a heavy stone roll with a flat stone platter.

USE FOR
Duck salmi (see page 79)

INGREDIENTS
1 (10 grams) **cinnamon stick**
10 cloves
3 dried red chillies
2 cloves garlic
1½ tablespoons vegetable oil

PREPARATION
Roast the cinnamon and cloves without oil in a frying pan (stirring often) or in the oven at 180° Celsius (356°F) until they become fragrant.

Combine all the ingredients and grind with a mortar and pestle until the ingredients become a paste.

Alternatively you can use a food processor.

Place the paste in an airtight container.

You can keep the paste refrigerated for at least two weeks.

VANILLA SUGAR

MADAGASCAR

YIELD
5 cups

LEVEL OF DIFFICULTY
Easy

TIME
5 minutes

TAGS
Make ahead

The vanilla plant [Orchidaceae], or more specifically Bourbon Madagascar vanilla plants [Vanilla planifolia] were originally introduced by Spanish explorers.

Now vanilla is among the biggest celebrities of the Indian Ocean and one of the most expensive spices in the world. Despite the price, the unique flavour of its seeds is hugely popular in local cuisine.

How to spot great quality vanilla? The dried fruits should be a bit sticky, have an amazing smell and should contain plenty of seeds.

CHEF'S NOTE
Whenever you have leftover vanilla pods from cooking, rinse and dry them, and use them to make vanilla sugar.

To make vanilla icing sugar, grind the vanilla sugar in a blender until it turns to powder, then sift to remove any lumps.

INGREDIENTS
20 to 30 vanilla pods (depends on quality)
1 kilogram (5 cups) **white sugar**

PREPARATION
Combine sugar and vanilla pods in an airtight container or a jar.

Store up to three months to enhance the flavour.

SIDES

'LET FRESH FRUITS AND VEGETABLES BE YOUR GUIDE'

~ Willibald Reinbacher ~

RIZ DES ÎLES
FRIED RICE WITH
SALTED FISH

MAURITIUS

YIELD
4 servings

LEVEL OF DIFFICULTY
Easy

TIME
Soak overnight, 30 minutes

TAGS
One-pot meal

CONTAINS
Chilli, fish, garlic, soy, wheat

Most of the fish found in the islands' local markets are caught in the waters around Rodrigues, an island neighbouring Mauritius. To conserve the fish population, fishermen have traditionally stopped fishing before the mating season and rather than having to go without fish, the catch is simply salted and air-dried to preserve it.

Therefore, salted fish is an ingredient that is indispensible in many traditional Mauritian meals and a vast number of local recipes call for "poisson salé".

My personal favourite is "riz des îles".

CHEF'S NOTE
The rice should be a leftover from the night before. The seasoning depends on the quality and taste of the salted fish, the fish sauce and salt may not be necessary.

INGREDIENTS
4 tablespoons cooking oil
100 grams (3.5 oz) **salted snook or cod,** soaked overnight then chopped
2 eggs
4 tablespoons chopped **onion**
2 tablespoons chopped **garlic**
2 teaspoons red chilli, chopped
400 grams (2 cups) **cooked rice** kept overnight
2 tablespoons diced **tomato**
1 teaspoon chopped **fresh thyme**

TO FINISH
Fish sauce to taste
Soy sauce to taste
Salt and **black pepper to taste**
4 tablespoons sliced **spring onion**

PREPARATION
Heat half the oil in a wok and fry the fish until crisp and brown in colour.

Add the eggs and stir-fry until they have a scrambled egg-like texture.

Remove all from the wok and set aside.

Heat the remaining oil and brown the onion and garlic. Add the red chilli.

Add the rice, tomato and thyme, then toss well.

To finish, return the egg and fish to the wok. Season to taste.

Add the spring onion just before serving.

RAVITATO SY VOANJO
CASSAVA LEAVES
WITH PEANUTS
MADAGASCAR

YIELD
4 servings
LEVEL OF DIFFICULTY
Easy
TIME
1 hour

TAGS
Gluten-free, vegan
CONTAINS
Chilli, garlic, peanuts

Cassava [Euphorbiaceae], commonly known as manioc or tapioca, is a root vegetable used in many recipes in the Indian Ocean and one of the leading sources of carbohydrates.

Cassava flour is used to make gluten-free bread or cakes. The root is either cooked in coconut milk to make sweets or boiled to eat with chutneys.

The leaf of the cassava is used in many households to make a hearty bouillon or, like in this recipe, as a side dish or a vegan option enjoyed on its own.

CHEF'S NOTE
The consistency should be like creamed spinach; add more stock or water if it becomes too dry. You can substitute wild garlic for the cassava leaves. If you cannot find fenugreek [Fabaceae] leaves, just omit them.

SERVE WITH
Steamed rice

INGREDIENTS
100 grams (3 cups) **cassava leaves,** cleaned
100 grams (¾ cup) **raw peanuts,** peeled
4 tablespoons peanut oil
20 grams (1½ tablespoons) **garlic,** chopped
1 teaspoon ginger powder
1 teaspoon fennel seed powder
1 teaspoon fenugreek leaves
1 teaspoon red chilli powder
1 pinch brown sugar
Salt to taste

TO FINISH
Peanuts, fried or roasted

PREPARATION
Bring water to a boil in a soup pot. Blanch the cassava leaves for a few seconds in the boiling water. Drain and quench the leaves in iced water. Keep 100 ml (½ cup) cooking water as stock for later. Drain and chop the leaves into pieces.

Grind the peanuts in a food processor.

Heat the oil in a saucepan over medium heat and gently sweat off the garlic.

Add all the spices and sauté for a few minutes until fragrant.

Add the cassava leaves, peanuts and cassava leaf stock. Bring all to a slow boil and simmer for approximately 30 minutes over low heat until the leaves lose their bitterness. Finally, add the brown sugar and season with salt.

To finish, garnish with the peanuts.

SATINI REKIN
SHARK CHUTNEY

SEYCHELLES

YIELD
4 servings

LEVEL OF DIFFICULTY
Easy

TIME
45 minutes

TAGS
Gluten-free

CONTAINS
Fish

Despite the controversy about shark fishing and sharks in general, sharks live in Seychelles territorial waters in great diversity; their breeding grounds have been established by the artisanal fishermen and shark fishing is an integral part of Seychellois culture.

Shark chutney is not only a delicacy in the Seychellois cuisine – it is as real as the Seychelles can get.

CHEF'S NOTE
You can substitute cod for the shark and tamarind paste for the bilimbi. If you like, you can add chopped coriander and sliced green chilli as a garnish.

SERVE WITH
Lentils, roti or rice

INGREDIENTS

500 grams (1.1 lb) **shark fillet** or cod
5 tablespoons cooking oil
100 grams (½ cup) **white onion,** sliced
2 tablespoons turmeric powder
50 ml (3½ tablespoons) **lime juice**
50 grams (4 tablespoons) peeled, seeded and chopped **bilimbi**
Salt and **pepper to taste**

PREPARATION

Gently boil the fish in water until cooked. Let the fish cool, then remove the skin and mash with a fork.

In a frying pan, heat the oil over medium heat and sweat off the onions.

Add the turmeric and the mashed shark, stir well.

Add the lime juice and bilimbi, mix well and season with salt and pepper.

CHILLI PASTE
COCONUT CHUTNEY
PAPAYA CHUTNEY

VARIOUS ISLANDS

YIELD
1 jar
LEVEL OF DIFFICULTY
Easy
TIME
20 minutes per recipe

TAGS
Gluten-free, make ahead, vegan
CONTAINS
Chilli, coconut, garlic, mustard

CHILLI PASTE

Chilli paste is a must for any meal on the Islands of the Indian Ocean. There are many family recipes. This is the one I like the most, because of the sweetness of the oranges and apples.

SERVE WITH
Curries, noodles or rice

INGREDIENTS
100 grams (1 cup) **green and red chillies**, roughly cut
1 **orange**, peeled, roughly cut
1 **lemon**, peeled, roughly cut
3 tablespoons chopped **garlic**
1 **apple**, roughly cut with skin on
2 tablespoons **white vinegar**
2 tablespoons **vegetable oil**
Salt to taste

PREPARATION
Combine all the ingredients in a bowl and marinate for one hour at room temperature.

Blend the mixture in a food processor and season to taste.

COCONUT TAMARIND CHUTNEY

This is one of the most popular chutneys to serve for breakfast or any snacks during the day. The mint and coconut in combination with coriander gives it an amazingly fresh touch.

SERVE WITH
Dhal puri (see page 155), roti

INGREDIENTS
100 grams (3.5 oz) **coconut**, its flesh grated (or frozen if not available)
2 tablespoons **tamarind paste**
2 tablespoons chopped **mint**
2 tablespoons chopped **coriander** (cilantro)
1 tablespoon **mustard seeds**, roasted
1 tablespoon **mustard oil** (if not available use vegetable oil)
1 gram (5 pieces) **curry leaves**, fried in a pan
Dried chilli to taste

PREPARATION
Combine all the ingredients with a mortar and pestle, or in a blender or food processor, .

Add some water until you get a paste-like consistency. Season to taste.

GREEN PAPAYA CHUTNEY

Great in salads, curries and to use as a tenderizer for the meat of the octopus, because it contains an enzyme called papain. The sweet spice of the green papaya makes it delicious.

SERVE WITH
Curries

INGREDIENTS
200 grams (2 cups) grated **green papaya**
3 tablespoons **olive oil**
60 grams (¼ cup) **red onion**, sliced
2 **garlic cloves**, chopped
50 ml (3½ tablespoons) **lime juice** to taste
Chilli, sliced
Salt and **black pepper** to taste

PREPARATION
Sprinkle the papaya with salt and let it rest for 15 minutes, then squeeze the water out of the papaya. Heat the oil in a small frying pan on medium heat.

Sweat off the onion and garlic in olive oil.

Add the papaya, lime juice, sliced chilli and season with salt and pepper.

Cook over medium heat tossing until the papaya is slightly wilted.

BANBUKEYLU HARISA
BREADFRUIT CURRY WITH
SMOKED TUNA

MALDIVES

YIELD
4 servings
LEVEL OF DIFFICULTY
Easy
TIME
40 minutes

TAGS
One-pot meal, smoke
CONTAINS
Chilli, coconut, dairy, fish

Traditional Maldivian cuisine is based on three main items and their derivatives: coconut, fish and starches. This recipe includes all the above; coconut cream, their plentiful tuna, which is smoked in this recipe, and the breadfruit.

CHEF'S NOTE
If you cannot find pandan leaf, use pandan extract. You can substitute the breadfruit with sweet potato and the smoked tuna with any other smoked fish.

INGREDIENTS
1 tablespoon **ghee** (or clarified butter)
50 grams (⅓ cup) **white onion,** chopped
20 grams (2½ tablespoons) **ginger,** chopped
1 **pandan leaf,** chopped
5 **curry leaves**
1 teaspoon **turmeric powder**
1 teaspoon **chilli,** chopped
200 grams (1½ cups) **breadfruit,**
peeled and cut into cubes
200 ml (¾ cup) **coconut cream**
50 grams (1.5 oz) **smoked tuna,** sliced

TO FINISH
1 **lemon,** squeezed
Salt to taste

PREPARATION
Heat the ghee in a frying pan over medium heat.

Add the onion and fry until golden brown in colour.

Add the ginger, pandan leaf, curry leaves, turmeric and chilli, then fry gently for another two minutes.

Add the breadfruit cubes, coconut cream and smoked tuna, then cook gently until the breadfruit is tender.

To finish, add the lemon juice and season with salt.

BRINJAL
SPICY EGGPLANT
INDONESIA

YIELD
4 servings

LEVEL OF DIFFICULTY
Easy

TIME
20 minutes

TAGS
Vegan

CONTAINS
Chilli, garlic, soy

Eggplant is famous in Indonesian cuisine and is everybodys favourite. There are even songs written about this beautiful vegetable. Eggplant is perfect for your meatless Monday. This is one of my favourite eggplant dishes: sweet, sour and very spicy. Enjoy!

CHEF'S NOTE
If you cannot find "Ketjap Manis", mix two tablespoons regular soy sauce with 1 tablespoon brown sugar.

SERVE WITH
Steamed rice

INGREDIENTS
500 grams (2 cups) **eggplant,** chopped into 3 cm (1.2 in) chunks
1 tablespoon tamarind paste
3 tablespoons Ketjap Manis
3 tablespoons water
1 tablespoon lime juice
1 tablespoon "Sambal Oelek"
1 tablespoon cooking oil
2 medium red onions, sliced
2 tablespoons chopped **garlic**
70 grams (⅓ cup) **tomato,** diced

TO FINISH
1 tablespoon coriander (cilantro), slivered
Salt to taste

PREPARATION
In a bowl marinate the eggplant with the tamarind paste, Ketjap Manis, water, lime juice and Sambal Oelek for at least one hour. Stir the eggplant in its marinade from time to time, then drain the eggplant and keep the marinade for later.

Heat the oil in a wok (or frying pan). Fry the onion and garlic until golden in colour.

Add the tomato and eggplant mixture to the pan. Cook, stirring occasionally, until the eggplant is soft. Depending on the quality of the eggplant, add water if necessary during the cooking process. Add the marinade, stir and cook for a few minutes until the dish has a stew-like consistency.

To finish, add the coriander and season with salt.

SWEET & SOUR SALAD
MAURITIUS

YIELD
4 servings

LEVEL OF DIFFICULTY
Easy

TIME
20 minutes

TAGS
Make ahead, raw, vegan

CONTAINS
Chilli, mustard

From tropical fruit to all kinds of vegetables, farmers grow nearly everything we need to live, and thanks to the year-round mild, tropical climate, farms have a constant cycle, ensuring a constant supply of fresh, tasty and healthy greens.

I dedicate this recipe to the Aquacasian farmers.

CHEF'S NOTE
The star of the dish is the sweet and sour dressing; it can be used for any salad, even with fish, chicken or seafood. You can prepare the dressing and salad ingredients in advance and finish just before serving.

DRESSING
1 tablespoon **Dijon® mustard**
30 ml (2 tablespoons) **lemon juice**
20 ml (1½ teaspoons) **sweet chilli sauce**
30 ml (2 tablespoons) **white vinegar**
15 ml (1 tablespoon) **walnut oil**
15 ml (1 tablespoon) **corn oil**
Salt and **pepper** to taste

SALAD
200 grams (1½ cups) **palm heart,** sliced
200 grams (1 cup) **sweet papaya,** cut into cubes
50 grams (¼ cup) **red onion,** thinly sliced into rings
100 grams (3 cups) **lettuce,** roughly cut
10 grams (¼ cup) **coriander** (cilantro) leaves
50 grams (¼ cup) **tomato,** cut into cubes

PREPARATION
For the dressing combine the mustard, lemon juice, sweet chilli sauce and vinegar in a small bowl.

Slowly whisk in the oils to emulsify the dressing, and season with salt and pepper.

To finish the salad, mix all salad ingredients and toss with the dressing.

POMME DE TERRE ET TI POIS
POTATO & PEAS

MAURITIUS

YIELD
4 servings
LEVEL OF DIFFICULTY
Easy
TIME
30 minutes

TAGS
Vegan
CONTAINS
Chilli, garlic

Mauritius produces more than 20,000 tons of potatoes annually; that is a lot of potatoes for a population of one million residents.

Naturally, there is a variety of local potato dishes; potato chutneys, curries with potatoes, potato masala and salads just to name a few.

This recipe is one of my favourites to roll into my "dhal puri".

CHEF'S NOTE
Adding a teaspoon of whole cumin seeds while cooking the onion gives an additional interesting note to the dish.

SERVE WITH
"Dhal puri" (see page 155) and coconut chutney (see page 127)

INGREDIENTS
2 tablespoons cooking oil
50 grams (⅓ cup) **white onion,** chopped
4 tablespoons garlic, chopped
4 tablespoons ginger, finely julienned
100 grams (½ cup) **tomato,** diced
200 grams (1 cup) **potato,**
peeled and cut into cubes
100 ml (½ cup) **vegetable stock**
4 thyme sprigs
1 tablespoon chopped, **dry chilli**

TO FINISH
100 grams (¾ cup) **green peas,** cooked
Salt and **pepper to taste**

PREPARATION
Heat the oil over medium heat in a casserole pan. Gently sweat off the onion, garlic and ginger.

Add the tomato, potatoes, stock, thyme and chilli. Bring to a boil, reduce heat and simmer with a lid on until the potatoes are tender.

To finish, add the peas, season with salt and pepper.

SNACKS

'YOU DON'T NEED
A SILVER FORK
TO EAT GOOD FOOD'

~ Paul Prudhomme ~

MKATRA FOUTRA
COCONUT BREAD
WITH SESAME
COMOROS

YIELD
4 servings
LEVEL OF DIFFICULTY
Medium
TIME
1 hour, 40 minutes

TAGS
No bake bread
CONTAINS
Coconut, egg, dairy, sesame, wheat

There is literally no dairy industry on the Comoros. So "mkatra foutra" bread, most likely introduced by Arabian traders, is made with coconut milk instead, lending it a very unique taste.

Eat hot or cold with soup, stew, fried fish or meat.

SERVE WITH
"Cabri masale" (see page 87)

INGREDIENTS

2.5 grams (1 teaspoon) **dry yeast**
2 cl (4 teaspoons) lukewarm **water**
200 grams (1½ cups) **white flour**
1 egg
1 pinch of salt
190 ml (¾ cup) **coconut milk**

TO FINISH

3 tablespoons butter, melted
Sesame seeds, to sprinkle

PREPARATION

Dissolve the yeast in a small bowl with the water. Combine the flour, yeast, egg and salt in an electric mixing bowl.

Add the coconut milk and beat for approximately four minutes until the dough has a sticky and elastic texture.

Cover the dough with cling film and allow to proof at room temperature for approximately one hour. The dough should rise slightly and little bubbles should form.

Heat a non-stick pan over low heat. Sprinkle some sesame seeds into the pan.

Using two wet spoons, spoon the dough in portion-sized dollops into the pan.

Before flipping the cakes, sprinkle some sesame on the top of the coconut breads.

Brush generously with melted butter on both sides, keep flipping and cook over low heat until both sides are golden brown.

Before serving, let the loaves rest on kitchen paper to absorb some of the butter.

KATLES
SPICED BEEF AND
POTATO PATTIES
MADAGASCAR

YIELD
4 servings
LEVEL OF DIFFICULTY
Medium
TIME
45 minutes

TAGS
Gluten-free
CONTAINS
Chilli, egg, garlic, meat

"Katles" originate from Indian cuisine and have become a tremendously popular snack in Malagasy cuisine. Usually made with beef, they can also be prepared with any other meat or fish and, of course, as a purely vegetarian version.

CHEF'S NOTE
If the dough is too moist before frying, add bread crumbs to more easily form patties.

PATTIES
100 grams (½ cup) **potato**
50 grams (3 tablespoons) **white onion,** chopped
20 grams (3 tablespoons) **ginger,** grated
20 grams (2 tablespoons) **garlic,** chopped
200 grams (7 oz) **ground beef**
1 **egg**
1 tablespoon **curry powder**
2 tablespoons **thyme,** chopped
2 tablespoons **chives,** chopped
2 tablespoons **coriander** (cilantro), chopped
Salt and **pepper** to taste
3 tablespoons **cooking oil**

MASALA
1 **tomato**
2 tablespoons diced **white onion**
1 teaspoon chopped **chilli**
1 teaspoon chopped **coriander** (cilantro)
1 **lemon,** squeezed
Salt to taste
"Chaat masala" to taste (see page 109)

PREPARATION
Peel the potatoes and boil them in salted water until soft. Add the tomato for the masala to the water for one minute, which will enable you to peel the tomato easily.

Remove the tomato and set aside for the masala. Drain the potatoes and let them cool, which releases their moisture.

Mash the potatoes with a fork in a bowl and add all remaining ingredients.

Mix until it all forms a firm dough. Season to taste and form patties to your desired size and set aside. This is easiest done with your hands.

For the masala, peel the tomato (which was blanched in the boiling potato water for one minute). Remove the seeds and dice the tomato. You need four tablespoons of peeled, seeded and diced tomato. In a small bowl combine all remaining masala ingredients and season to taste with salt and **"chaat masala"** (see page 109).

Heat the oil in a frying pan over medium to high heat. Fry the patties on both sides until golden brown in colour.

Serve with the masala.

MASROSHI
STUFFED FLAT-BREAD

MALDIVES

YIELD
4 servings
LEVEL OF DIFFICULTY
Medium
TIME
2 hours

TAGS
No bake bread
CONTAINS
Chilli, coconut, fish, wheat

"Masroshi" is the most popular afternoon or breakfast snack in the Maldives.

A very simple stuffed flat-bread with smoked tuna, coconut dough and cooked on a griddle or hot stone. Yummy!

CHEF'S NOTE
You can substitute the smoked tuna with any other smoked fish.

DOUGH
300 grams (2½ cups) **white flour**
½ teaspoon salt
25 ml (5 teaspoons) **vegetable oil**
50 ml (3½ tablespoons) **warm water**

STUFFING
150 grams (5 oz) **smoked tuna,** chopped
50 grams (½ cup) **coconut flakes**
1 tablespoon chilli, chopped
1 white onion, finely sliced
3 curry leaves, chopped
½ teaspoon turmeric powder
1 lemon, juiced
Salt and **pepper to taste**

PREPARATION
Mix the flour, salt and oil in a bowl. Then slowly add the water while mixing, later kneading the dough until soft, but not sticky. You might not need all the water or perhaps a bit more. Cover the dough and leave to rest for about one hour at room temperature.

Combine all the stuffing ingredients in a bowl and mix well. Season to taste with the salt and pepper.

Divide the dough into 70 gram (⅓ cup) balls.

Flatten each ball with your palm, add a generous spoon of the stuffing and seal with your fingers, making sure there are no holes in the dough.

Sprinkle your kitchen counter with flour and gently roll each ball with a pastry or dough roller into a round circle of approximately 1 cm (0.4 in) thickness.

Fry the "masroshis" on a hot griddle or over medium heat in a non-stick pan.

You might have to fry them in batches, turning frequently to ensure that they do not burn.

Fry to a golden brown colour.

PIMENT FARCI
STUFFED CHILLI PEPPERS

MAURITIUS

YIELD
16 peppers

LEVEL OF DIFFICULTY
Medium

TIME
45 minutes

TAGS
Fry, gluten-free

CONTAINS
Chilli, egg, garlic, fish

The chilli pepper is called "piment cari" on the island. It is best to choose a large green chilli. Large chillies are normally less spicy than the smaller ones, but if it is still too hot for your taste, prepare this recipe with small red peppers [Capsicum].

CHEF'S NOTE
You can substitute the tuna with any other ingredient; make sure you cook the stuffing before filling the chillies with it. Corn flour is also called corn meal; do not substitute it with cornstarch.

SERVE WITH
Drinks

INGREDIENTS
2 tablespoons cooking oil
30 grams (¼ cup) **white onion,** chopped
15 grams (1 tablespoon) **garlic,** chopped
300 grams (10.5 oz) **canned tuna**
1 lemon, squeezed
2 tablespoons chopped
coriander (cilantro) leaves
Salt and **pepper to taste**
16 piment cari (Mauritian chilli peppers)
or use any green peppers
that are not too spicy

TO FINISH
1 egg, beaten in a small bowl
125 grams (¾ cup) **corn flour**
1 teaspoon salt
Some water
Oil for deep-frying

PREPARATION
Heat the oil over medium heat in a frying pan. Sweat off the onion and garlic until soft and add the tuna. Mix and make sure the tuna breaks apart into small pieces.

Add the lemon juice, coriander and season with salt and pepper.

Let the stuffing cool.

Carefully cut the chillies near the tail ¾ through, remove the seeds, stuff with the tuna and close again with the tail.

Heat the frying oil in a small saucepan or fryer. In a bowl whisk the egg, corn flour and salt with some water to form a smooth batter.

When the oil is ready for frying, carefully dip the chillies in the batter and deep-fry in the oil until crisp and golden brown. Work in batches, to avoid overcrowding the pan.

Let the fried chilli rest on kitchen paper and serve hot.

GÂTEAU PIMENT
CHILLI AND DHAL FRITTERS

MAURITIUS

YIELD
4 servings
LEVEL OF DIFFICULTY
Medium
TIME
Soak overnight, 1 hour

TAGS
Fry, gluten-free, vegan
CONTAINS
Chilli

Street food is an old tradition on the island and is celebrated proudly.

As soon as you travel a bit off the beaten path, you can be certain to find a little shack serving one or more tasty snacks to whet your appetite.

You will certainly find "Gâteau piment" or "Mauritian dhal fritters", one of the most popular street food snacks on the island.

To avoid confusion: yellow split peas, dhal (or dal) and yellow lentils are all the same thing.

CHEF'S NOTE
Add some cumin powder to the pea mixture for a more complex flavour.

CHILLI CAKES
200 grams (1 cup) **yellow split peas**
1 red onion, finely chopped
3 tablespoons coriander (cilantro), chopped
3 tablespoons spring onion, finely sliced
2 tablespoons chopped **green chilli**
(or more if you like it spicy)
Salt to taste
Oil for deep-frying

TOMATO CHUTNEY
3 medium-sized tomatoes, roughly chopped
3 tablespoons chopped **white onion**
1 teaspoon chopped **garlic**
2 tablespoons chopped **green chilli**
3 tablespoons coriander (cilantro) leaves
Salt to taste

PREPARATION
Wash the split peas, place in a bowl and cover them with plenty of water. Soak overnight in the refrigerator.

Drain the split peas and blend in a food processor. Make sure not to over blend; the mixture should remain chunky.

In a bowl mix the peas and add all the remaining ingredients to form a paste. Season with salt.

For the tomato chutney, combine all the ingredients and blend in a food processor. Season to taste.

Heat the oil for deep-frying in a small saucepan or fryer at 160° Celsius (320°F). Shape small balls with your hands or two spoons and deep-fry until golden brown on all sides.

Deep-fry the cakes in batches to avoid overcrowding the frying pan or fryer.

Allow the cakes to cool slightly on kitchen paper before serving them with the tomato chutney.

DHAL PURI
LENTIL FLAT-BREAD

MAURITIUS

YIELD
About 20 flat-breads

LEVEL OF DIFFICULTY
Medium

TIME
Soak overnight; 1 hour, 30 minutes

TAGS
No-bake bread, vegan

CONTAINS
Wheat

Some countries put their national dish on their flying colours – if Mauritius wanted to do that too, a "dhal puri" (also dal or dholl puri) would proudly fly over the presidential palace.

Dhal puri is pure pleasure for your taste buds and can accompany anything and be eaten at any time.

CHEF'S NOTE
Like many "roti" recipes, it takes a lot of practice to obtain the perfect dhal puri. Once you get the hang of it, it is very easy and fun to make.

SERVE WITH
The best thing about dhal puri is that it can be served with savoury or sweet dishes.

INGREDIENTS
300 grams (1⅓ cup) **yellow dhal** (lentils), washed and soaked overnight
1½ litre (6⅓ cups) water
1 tablespoon ground cumin
1 tablespoon turmeric powder
3 tablespoons vegetable oil
1 teaspoon salt
1 kilogram (4 cups) **white flour**
2 teaspoons salt
Flour to dust
Cooking oil to brush on pan

PREPARATION
Boil the drained lentils in a soup pot with the water, cumin, turmeric, vegetable oil and salt until they are very soft and well cooked. Skim off any froth during the boiling. Strain the boiling liquid in a separate container, cool and set aside for the dough. Briefly mix the lentils in a food processor, the lentils should remain chunky.

In a bowl combine the flour and salt with approximately 400 ml (2½ cups) of the lentil liquid and knead to a firm dough. Add the liquid gradually; you might need a bit less or more liquid. Prepare 50 to 70 grams (¼ cup) sized balls, cover them with a kitchen towel and let rest for 15 minutes.

With your thumb press a hole into each ball and form a small cup. Fill the cup in your hand with a tablespoon of the crushed lentils. Close the cup, pinching the dough together and making sure that there is no air inside the ball. Dust a wooden board with flour, and with a rolling pin, roll each ball as thin as possible into round flat-breads.

Heat a "tawa", crepe pan or a large non-stick pan over medium to high heat. Brush the surface with oil and cook the puris, flipping continuously after a few seconds to avoid browning. Also brush the puris directly with oil if necessary. Cook them until they slightly puff up and change colour. You do not want the puris to get too brown.

KOTHU STIR-FRIED ROTI
WITH EGG AND VEGETABLES

SRI LANKA

YIELD
4 servings

LEVEL OF DIFFICULTY
Easy

TIME
30 minutes

TAGS
One-pot meal

CONTAINS
Chilli, egg, garlic, wheat

"Kothu roti" originates from "kothu parotta", a very popular, high-energy, Southern Indian roadside snack.

It is an amazing experience to see these being made roadside, in one of the countless variations.

The vegetarian variation in this recipe is perfect for breakfast, lunch or as a tasty snack in between.

CHEF'S NOTE
If you want to eat this dish as a main course just double the recipe and add any type of meat or fish to your liking. Even "kothu" with cheese is a popular variety.

INGREDIENTS
2 tablespoons cooking oil
1 teaspoon chopped **ginger**
1 teaspoon chopped **garlic**
1 teaspoon curry powder
100 grams (1 cup) **carrots,** julienned
50 grams (½ cup) **cabbage,** shredded
50 grams (⅓ cup) **leek,** thinly sliced
2 eggs, beaten in a small bowl
200 grams (2 cups) **roti,** cut into pieces (use any old roti from an Indian restaurant)
1 teaspoon chopped **green chilli**
Salt and **pepper to taste**

TO FINISH
Spring onions, finely sliced

PREPARATION
Heat the oil in a wok. Add the ginger and garlic, stir-fry until soft, but not brown.

Add the curry powder and fry until fragrant.

Add the carrots, cabbage and leek and fry until all is cooked, but not entirely soft. Remove all from the wok and set aside.

Heat the wok again with some oil.

Add the beaten eggs and chillies and fry until the eggs begin to firm, then add the roti pieces and continue frying.

Return the vegetables to the wok and season with salt and pepper.

To finish, garnish the dish with the spring onions.

DEEP-FRIED
JACKFRUIT SEEDS

SRI LANKA

YIELD
4 servings
LEVEL OF DIFFICULTY
Medium
TIME
45 minutes

TAGS
Fry, gluten-free, vegan
CONTAINS
Chilli, coconut

It is believed that the jackfruit tree [Artocarpus heterophyllus], or simply "jak", was discovered (and named) by Portuguese explorers and brought to the islands by Indian traders. Given the fact that this tree is now widely cultivated throughout the Indian Ocean region, they obviously are perfectly adapted to their new habitat.

The flesh of the fruit has a sweet aroma with a fruity note – comparable to a combination of banana, mango and pineapple.

The seeds are reminiscent of Brazil nuts and when cooked make a fantastic snack.

CHEF'S NOTE
You can substitute cashew nuts for the jackfruit seeds. Just skip the boiling step at the beginning.

SERVE WITH
Drinks

INGREDIENTS

200 grams (3.5 oz) **jackfruit seeds**
Oil for deep-frying
80 grams (¼ cup) **white onion,** finely sliced
50 grams (½ cup) **coconut flakes**
Salt to taste
Chilli flakes to taste

PREPARATION

Cook the jackfruit seeds in boiling water for about 15 minutes until they are soft.

Drain the seeds, remove the shells and cut into halves.

Heat the frying oil in a fryer or small saucepan and fry the seeds until they are nicely browned and crispy.

Remove the seeds from the oil and drain on absorbent kitchen paper.

Then deep-fry the sliced onion until golden brown.

Heat a frying pan over medium heat and toast the coconut flakes until they change colour and become fragrant.

To finish, place the jackfruit seeds in a bowl and mix with the onion and coconut flakes.

Season with salt and chilli flakes.

FISH CUTLETS
FISH CAKES WITH
TOMATO CHUTNEY

SRI LANKA

YIELD
6 servings

LEVEL OF DIFFICULTY
Medium

TIME
1 hour

TAGS
Fry

CONTAINS
Chilli, egg, fish, wheat

Fish cutlets are served as a snack at any Sri Lankan party and especially on game day (meaning cricket and rugby).

While every Sri Lankan family has their own version of these fish cakes with their own special spices, they all share the same core ingredients.

They can be prepared with any cooked or steamed, firm, flaky, white fish, fresh or canned. Mackerel or tuna work well as options.

CHEF'S NOTE
If you cannot find curry leaves, just omit them.

SERVE WITH
Drinks

INGREDIENTS

150 grams (¾ cup) potato
150 grams (5 oz) fish fillet
50 grams (⅓ cup) red onion, chopped
20 grams (4 tablespoons)
green chilli, chopped
5 grams (25 pieces) curry
leaves, very finely sliced
½ teaspoon ground black pepper
½ teaspoon chilli powder
½ teaspoon cumin powder
Salt to taste
Lime juice to taste
4 tablespoons white flour
2 eggs, beaten
70 grams (½ cup) bread crumbs
Oil for deep-frying

TOMATO & CUMIN CHUTNEY

1 tablespoon cooking oil
10 curry leaves
1 medium-sized red onion, chopped
4 large tomatoes, diced
1 teaspoon red chilli powder (according to your preferred spiciness)
1½ teaspoons cumin powder
A pinch of salt
A pinch of sugar

PREPARATION

For the chutney, heat the oil in a frying pan and fry the curry leaves until fragrant. Add the onions and sweat off until they are tender, but not coloured. Add all the remaining ingredients and stir-fry until they reach a chutney-like consistency. Let cool. If you prefer, you can blend the chutney in a food processor to get a finer consistency.

For the fish cakes, first peel, then boil the potatoes in salted water until cooked. Drain the potatoes and let cool so that the moisture evaporates. At the same time, cook the fish in a little oil or your preferred cooking method.

Mash the potatoes in a large bowl; add the fish and all remaining ingredients along with the cumin powder. Combine until it all becomes a firm mass. Season to taste by adding the salt and lime juice.

Prepare three medium bowls; one each with the flour, eggs and breadcrumbs. Season the breadcrumbs with salt.

To make the fish cakes, use your hands to prepare croquet-style cakes. Then dust them with flour, dip them in the egg wash and finally coat them with bread crumbs. Place on a plate.

Heat the oil in a saucepan or a fryer at 180° Celsius (355°F). Deep-fry the fish cakes until golden. Place the cakes on kitchen paper and serve warm with the chutney.

SUGAR CANE PRAWNS

INDONESIA

YIELD
8 skewers

LEVEL OF DIFFICULTY
Easy

TIME
30 minutes, 1 hour resting

TAGS
Gluten-free

CONTAINS
Egg, garlic, fish, seafood

Sugar cane [Poaceae] is more than just its sweet juice, it is still an important economic pillar for some countries in the Indian Ocean. Indonesia counts among the top ten producers globally.

Sugar cane has naturally found its way into the local cuisine, even if it is merely as the skewer that makes the difference.

CHEF'S NOTE
You can substitute sugar cane with bamboo skewers.

SERVE WITH
Drinks or as a starter

INGREDIENTS
500 grams (1.1 lb) **raw prawns** (shrimp), cleaned and peeled
1 egg white
2 cloves garlic, chopped
2 tablespoons chopped **coriander** (cilantro)
2 tablespoons kaffir lime leaves, very finely julienned
2 tablespoons fish sauce
Salt to taste
Sugar cane to make **8 skewers**

DIPPING SAUCE
4 tablespoons fish sauce
1 small red chilli, chopped
1 tablespoon roasted peanuts, chopped
2 teaspoons liquid honey
1 tablespoon chopped coriander (cilantro)
1 tablespoon lime juice

PREPARATION
Lightly chop the prawns in a food processor. There should still be chunks of prawns visible. In a bowl mix the prawn paste well with the egg white. Add all the remaining ingredients. Mix well and season to taste.

Peel the sugar cane and cut the core into 10 cm (4 in) long and approximately 1.5 cm (0.6 in) wide skewers. Make eight pieces.

Divide the prawn mixture into eight portions. With wet hands mould the prawn mixture around the sugar cane, covering approximately ⅔ of the skewers. Cover the skewers with foil and let set in the refrigerator for one hour.

To make the dipping sauce, combine all the ingredients in a bowl and set aside.

To finish the skewers, you can steam them in a bamboo or metal steamer until the colour changes and the prawn mix is cooked in the middle. Or bake them in the oven at 180° Celsius (355°F) for a few minutes. Or deep-fry them in oil to a light brown colour.

Serve with the dipping sauce.

DAMPER BREAD
BUSHMAN BREAD
AUSTRALIA

YIELD
1 loaf

LEVEL OF DIFFICULTY
Medium

TIME
1 hour

TAGS
Bake

CONTAINS
Dairy, wheat

Damper bread or bush bread is an iconic dish of the travelling native tribes of Australia who walked through remote areas for weeks, sometimes months, with few rations, just essentials.

Normally the bread is cooked in the ashes of a campfire or in a thick walled iron camp oven (Dutch oven).

Damper bread does not taste like anything you have ever baked before.

CHEF'S NOTE
You can change the flavour of the bread to your liking by adding spices (such as cumin, cardamom, curry powder or just garlic paste) or by replacing the water with another liquid such as milk, buttermilk or any flavoured liquid.

SERVE WITH
BBQ or any meal

INGREDIENTS
250 grams (2 cups) **self-raising flour**
plus ½ **teaspoon salt**
or
(**250 grams** (2 cups) **white flour** plus
1½ **teaspoon salt** and
4 teaspoons baking powder)
25 grams (2 tablespoons) **unsalted butter**, cubed and softened
175 ml (¾ cup) **water**

PREPARATION
Combine the flour and salt in a stand mixer. Add the butter cubes and beat for one minute. Add the water slowly; you might not need all of it. Beat for around two minutes until a soft, non-sticky dough forms. Remove the dough from the mixer and work with your hands on a flour dusted surface for a few minutes until the dough is smooth. Form into a ball.

FOR BAKING IN AN OVEN
Heat the oven to 180° Celsius (355°F). Form the dough into a round flat disc and place on a greased baking tray. Slash the top crust with the tip of a serrated knife. Bake for approximately 35 to 40 minutes in the preheated oven until golden brown in colour. To know when the bread is ready, tap on the bottom of the loaf; it should sound hollow.

FOR CAMPFIRE COOKING
Grease a campfire oven (Dutch oven) and dust with flour. Place the dough in the oven and cover with a lid. Place the oven in your campfire and cover with hot ashes. Cook for approximately 40 minutes. To know when the bread is ready, tap on the bottom of the loaf; it should sound hollow.

'SOME PEOPLE HANDLE SWEETS BETTER'

As you are well aware, there are countless discussions and probably even more opinions about food and its ingredients. Some take very strict positions and try to lead every dinner conversation into a rally for their beliefs. I agree that too much of anything is unhealthy, but a little of what you fancy will not harm you.

You might ask yourself why people discuss food so passionately? Perhaps it is because for the first time in human history food has lost its vital component and become a commodity. Today it is a lifestyle choice and not just basic survival. These facts distract from the basic needs and satisfaction of food and its pure pleasure.

I understand and respect that the modern household has dramatically changed since the mechanisation of agriculture and industrialisation, and that the food industry adapted quickly to these trends, but this is also the main reason why we have lost our real connection to food and predominantly to its raw products and sources.

There are encouraging movements all around the globe that seek to return to nature and to learn more about how vegetables grow, how fish is caught and how animals are bred. Some, in fact, are getting back to basics to gain a deeper understanding of natural cycles and the impacts of mass production.

Of course, on a global scale, this is a drop in the ocean, but then again: nothing good comes easily and we should encourage this movement.

I strongly believe that we hold the key to the future of food for generations to come and that we can do something about the general misconception of what we mean by a healthy diet, which should not just exclude certain items but should also be properly balanced: fibre, vitamins, minerals and proteins should come from fresh, seasonal, raw products in food prepared by you!

My adventures around the Indian Ocean taught me how easy it can actually be to prepare healthy, nutritious, and even more importantly, delicious dishes. All this with a minimal amount of time, effort and kitchen work. And once you become familiar with the spices, it gets even easier. I promise!

And yes, balance means that sugar (in moderation and in its most natural form – or simply fresh, seasonal and raw fruit) must be a part of what you eat. Let's face it: a proper guilty pleasure is the best possible way to round off a delicious meal.

Read on to see how easy it is to handle sweets!

SWEETS

'I EAT A LOT OF SALAD,
A LITTLE MEAT, AND SOME
FRUIT – THAT'S ALL

BUT I LOVE SWEETS'

~ Sophia Loren ~

COCONUT WITH LADO, NOUGAT & GÂTEAU

VARIOUS ISLANDS

YIELD
10-20 pieces each
LEVEL OF DIFFICULTY
Medium
TIME
30 minutes each

TAGS
Make ahead
CONTAINS
Coconut, dairy

LADO COCO

250 grams (2 cups) **finely grated fresh coconut** (or dry coconut powder)
225 grams (⅔ cup) **sweet condensed milk**
2.5 grams (1 teaspoon) **cardamom powder**
Grated coconut (or powder) **to dust**

PREPARATION

Combine all the ingredients in a bowl and form a firm dough.

With your hands, roll small balls to the preferred size.

Roll the balls on a plate with some coconut powder and coat the "lados" evenly. Keep refrigerated, but serve at room temperature.

CHEF'S NOTE

The firmness of the dough depends on the moisture of the coconut, adjust with either more condensed milk if the dough is too dry, or some additional coconut powder if it is too wet.

NOUGAT COCO

250 grams (2 cups) **finely grated fresh coconut**
400 grams (1⅔ cups) **white sugar**
50 ml (3½ tablespoons) **water**
1 **vanilla pod,** seeds scraped out (or vanilla essence)

PREPARATION

In a saucepan heat water and sugar gently over low heat. Do not stir, otherwise the sugar will crystallise. Keep over low heat until the sugar has a golden colour. Remain patient; at some point the sugar will become caramel; this takes at least 10 minutes.

Add the coconut slowly to the hot caramel and cook for another five minutes over low heat. Remove the pan from the heat and stir in the vanilla pod seeds.

To make the nougats, pour the mixture on to a greased baking tray (30 x 40 cm, 12 x 15.5 in) and spread evenly in a single layer around 1½ cm (0.6 in) thick.

Let cool and cut into squares.

CHEF'S NOTE

You can add a few teaspoons of rum while stirring in the coconut.

GÂTEAU COCO

250 ml (1 cup) **water**
375 grams (1¾ cups) **white sugar**
3 **vanilla pods**
150 grams (1½ cups) finely grated **fresh coconut**

PREPARATION

Heat the water with the sugar in a small saucepan and cook over low heat until the sugar is dissolved.

Cut the vanilla pods lengthwise into halves, use a spoon or knife to scrape out the seeds and add them to the sugar syrup.

Stir in the coconut flakes and cook until all liquid is absorbed.

With two spoons, form the mixture into cookie portions; place them on a tray and let them cool and set.

CHEF'S NOTE

To make grated coconut you need to first get the coconut out of the shell. Place the coconut in a preheated oven at 250° Celsius (480°F) wait until it cracks, then remove the hairy nut and break with a hammer. Remove the white meat, peel off the very thin brown skin and grate.

GODROGODRO
COCONUT & VANILLA
SPICE CAKE
MADAGASCAR

YIELD
1 cake

LEVEL OF DIFFICULTY
High

TIME
1 hour, 30 minutes, 3 hours to set

TAGS
Bake, make ahead, vegan

CONTAINS
Coconut, wheat

Sweets in the Indian Ocean region are different from anything you may be familiar with. While some of the ingredients might seem rather "old school", every single recipe I have collected is unique.

This is one of the most popular sweet treats in Madagascar: the "godrogodro" – a fantastic coconut and vanilla cake.

INGREDIENTS

400 grams (2 cups) **white sugar,** divided
90 ml (6 tablespoons) **water,** divided
1 litre (4 cups) **coconut milk**
500 grams (2½ cups) **fine semolina** (durum wheat flour)
3 grams (1½ teaspoons) **cinnamon powder**
2 vanilla pods, seeds scraped out (or vanilla essence)
2 grams (2 teaspoons) **nutmeg powder**
2 grams (1 teaspoon) **clove powder**

PREPARATION

In a large saucepan or soup pot heat half of the water with half of the sugar over low heat. Cook without stirring too frequently until the sugar becomes caramelised. Be careful not to burn the sugar.

Add the coconut milk very slowly to the caramel in batches, stirring well after each batch. If you add the milk too fast, the caramel will harden. Slowly whisk in the semolina. Then add all the spices. Stirring constantly, cook gently until the semolina is cooked and resembles a sticky paste. A heat-proof spatula works best to keep the paste from sticking to the pan. Remove the pan from the stove and pour into a round spring form and set aside.

Heat the oven to 200° Celsius (390°F).

Next prepare a second caramel in a small saucepan with the remaining water and sugar. Again heat over low to medium heat. Just as the sugar turns to a caramel pour it over the cake and spread evenly with a spatula. Do not worry about spreading the caramel perfectly as it will distribute itself during the baking process.

Bake the cake in a preheated oven for approximately 30 minutes until the caramel starts bubbling.

Allow to cool, then refrigerate for at least three hours to set before serving.

BANBUKEYO BONDIBAI
BREADFRUIT COOKED IN
COCONUT MILK
MALDIVES

YIELD
4 servings

LEVEL OF DIFFICULTY
Easy

TIME
30 minutes

TAGS
Gluten-free, vegan

CONTAINS
Coconut

According to oral tradition, the breadfruit plant was brought from Java to Sri Lanka by Dutch colonial rulers and not with the best intentions in mind. However, the rulers' plan to weaken the natives with the introduction of the fruit failed spectacularly – obviously. The locals simply cooked the fruit, mixed it with fresh coconut and, thanks to the fruit's high vitamin C content, perhaps it even made them stronger. From then on, the breadfruit's triumphal march spread throughout the Indian Ocean and now is grown more or less on every island and is considered a staple food.

The plant is not only valued for its fruit, but also for its light and sturdy timber, which is used for outrigger canoes and to build family homes.

Breadfruit is very rich in starch and when cooked, the taste is very similar to a potato or fresh bread.

CHEF'S NOTE
You can use sweet potato instead of breadfruit. If you do, reduce the sugar by half.

INGREDIENTS
2 (400 grams) **breadfruits,** diced into about 0.5 cm (0.2 in) cubes
200 ml (¾ cup) **water**
200 grams (1 cup) **white sugar**
100 grams (3.5 oz) **coconut cream**

PREPARATION
Bring the water to a boil in a saucepan and add the breadfruit. Cook until soft. Then drain it, rinse with water and return to the saucepan.

Over medium heat add the sugar, cover with a lid and cook until the sugar is dissolved and it all becomes a somewhat sticky mixture.

Add the coconut cream and simmer for a few minutes.

Serve the breadfruit warm.

LEMON GRASS SAGO
WITH MANGO
INDONESIA

YIELD
8 servings
LEVEL OF DIFFICULTY
Medium
TIME
1 hour, 2 hours to set

TAGS
Make ahead
CONTAINS
Dairy, eggs

The sago palm [Metroxylon sagu] has historically been the main source of starch in the tropical regions of Asia and is therefore of culinary importance and considered a staple food.

In Indonesia, "sago" starch is used, as in Western cuisine, to bake or is mixed with boiling water to make a paste.

CHEF'S NOTE
The volume of the cooked sago should be roughly equal to the amount of custard.

INGREDIENTS
80 grams (½ cup) **sago pearls** (or tapioca pearls)
250 ml (1 cup) **milk**
60 grams (½ cup) **white sugar**
35 grams (⅓ cup) **egg yolks**
30 grams (3 stems) **lemon grass**

TO FINISH
1 mango, diced

PREPARATION
Bring water to a boil in a soup pot. Add the sago or tapioca while stirring to keep it from sticking to the pot and gently simmer until the pearls are transparent and soft. This takes about 10–15 minutes, depending on the size of the pearls. Strain the pearls, rinse with cold water and set aside.

In a saucepan bring the milk to a slow boil. Cut the lemon grass stems in half and break each, in turn, again in half, which helps release the flavour during the cooking process. Add the lemon grass halves; lower the heat and let the lemon grass flavour infuse the milk for 15 minutes.

Beat the egg yolks and sugar until fluffy and light in colour. Strain the milk and slowly whisk it into the egg mixture.

Return the mixture to a clean pan and reheat again on medium heat, stirring continuously with a wooden spoon or spatula until the mass begins to thicken. This step requires some attention and patience. Take care not to overheat the mixture or else the eggs will curdle. After a couple of minutes the mixture will start to thicken. Put the mixture back into the mixing bowl, and over iced water continue to mix and cool the mass simultaneously for a couple of minutes. When the custard has cooled off, add the tapioca and mix well.

Carefully spoon the mixture into serving glasses or bowls. Cover and refrigerate for a couple of hours or overnight so that if becomes slightly firm.

To finish, garnish with mango or any fruit you prefer.

WATALAPPAM
JAGGERY PUDDING WITH CASHEW NUTS

SRI LANKA

YIELD
1 dish

LEVEL OF DIFFICULTY
Medium

TIME
1 hour

TAGS
Bake, gluten-free, make ahead

CONTAINS
Coconut, egg

The fabled spice producer, Sri Lanka, was a busy trading post for many centuries. Naturally, the mix of nations and influences of the British colonialists and their Indian neighbours added even more spice to the colourful mix that makes this cuisine very exciting.

"Watalappam" (in some areas "wat-alappan" or "vatlappam") was first introduced by the Malays. This pudding is a truly popular dessert and an extraordinary example of Sri Lankan culinary art.

"Jaggery" is crystalline sugar still enveloped in the cooked juice from which it is formed. In Indian stores it is called "jaggery" or "gur", while in Latin American stores it is called "piloncillo", "papelon" or "panela". Its flavour ranges from mild caramel to strong molasses.

INGREDIENTS

5 eggs
375 ml (1½ cups) **coconut milk**
125 grams (¾ cup) **jaggery,** grated or powder
2 grams (1 teaspoon) **cardamom powder**
1 gram (½ teaspoon) **cinnamon powder**
4 tablespoons cashew nuts

PREPARATION

Separate the egg whites from the egg yolks. In a bowl combine the egg yolks, coconut milk, jaggery, cardamom and cinnamon.

Heat the oven to 150° Celsius (300°F) and place a roasting pan or another large dish filled with water in the oven. This will serve as a water bath in which to cook the watalappam. Make sure that the dish with the watalappam fits in the pan and that there is not too much water in the pan.

Lightly beat the egg whites until slightly foamy, then gently fold them into the coconut mixture with a spatula.

Pour the mixture into an ovenproof dish or portion-sized small dishes and bake in the water bath for about 15 minutes. Then sprinkle with the cashew nuts and bake for another 15 minutes.

Serve warm or cold.

DHONKEYO KAJURU
DEEP-FRIED BANANA
DUMPLINGS

MALDIVES

YIELD
4 servings

LEVEL OF DIFFICULTY
Medium

TIME
30 minutes

TAGS
Fry, make ahead, vegan

CONTAINS
Coconut, wheat

As with most Maldivian recipes, coconut plays an important role in this dessert.

It is impossible to stroll through a farmers market on any of the Maldivian islands and not stumble upon at least one booth that sells this deep-fried banana cake. There you can watch the merchants grate, squeeze and press coconuts for their goodness (milk, flesh, oil), which is simply fascinating and makes them taste even better.

CHEF'S NOTE
The locals of the Maldives also use vanilla essence instead of rose water to flavour the dumplings.

INGREDIENTS

4 very ripe bananas
80 grams (⅓ cup) **white sugar**
150 grams (1 cup) **white flour**
70 grams (¾ cup) **grated coconut** (fresh or dried)
2 tablespoons rose water
oil for deep-frying

TO FINISH

Vanilla icing (see page 113)

PREPARATION

In a bowl, mash the bananas with a fork and combine with the sugar.

Add all the remaining ingredients and mix well.

Heat the oil in a small saucepan or fryer. With two spoons, form balls and deep-fry in batches until they are golden brown in colour. Remove the dumplings from the oil and let them rest on kitchen paper.

To finish, arrange the dumplings on a plate and with a sieve dust with the **vanilla icing** (see page 113).

KOBA AKONDRO
MADGASCAR

YIELD
4 small cakes

LEVEL OF DIFFICULTY
Medium

TIME
1 hour

TAGS
Gluten-free

CONTAINS
Peanuts

The local hero of Madagascan sweets is "koba akondro" (also known as "kobindravina"). This steamed banana and peanut cake is typically sold by local vendors in marketplaces and at gas stations.

It takes on different flavours when served hot or cold. Both are tasty and the perfect on-the-go treat!

CHEF'S NOTE
Use parchment paper if you cannot find banana leaves.

INGREDIENTS
Banana leaves for wrapping
3 ripe bananas
50 grams (⅓ cup) **rice flour**
25 grams (2 tablespoons) **brown sugar**
100 grams (⅔ cup) **raw peanuts,** roughly chopped in a blender
¼ tablespoon vanilla extract or seeds
2 tablespoons honey
String for tying

PREPARATION
In a large soup pot place the banana leaves in boiling water for a few seconds so they become soft. Quench the boiled leaves in iced water. Drain the leaves and pat dry with a paper towel.

Cut the banana leaves into 15 cm (6 in) squares. You need four squares.

In a bowl, mash the bananas with a fork and combine with all the remaining ingredients to make a thick batter.

Divide the banana mixture into four portions. Place each portion in the centre of a banana leaf. Fold each leaf into a parcel and tie closed with the string.

Arrange the parcels in a bamboo (or metal) steamer and gently steam over boiling water for about 25 minutes until the parcels feel firm.

Serve warm.

BAKED YOGHURT

SRI LANKA

YIELD
4 servings
LEVEL OF DIFFICULTY
Easy
TIME
2 hours

TAGS
Bake, gluten-free
CONTAINS
Dairy

Sri Lanka is a culinary paradise and the food is incredibly good. Many of the typical dishes are similar to Indian cuisine, which is why yoghurt is served with most meals.

Traditional families in rural areas still make their own yoghurt with the curd of cows' or buffalo milk. This is easier than you might think – and about as simple as this delicious and refreshing dessert.

A true crowd-pleaser.

SERVE WITH
Any fruit of your choice

INGREDIENTS

200 grams (¾ cup) **sweet condensed milk**
200 ml (¾ cup) **full fat cream**
3 vanilla pods
250 grams (1 cup) **plain yoghurt**

PREPARATION

Heat the oven to 100° Celsius (210°F).

Place a roasting pan or other large dish filled with water in the oven. This will serve as a water bath in which to cook the yoghurt. Make sure that the dish for the yoghurt fits the pan before heating and that there is not too much water in the pan.

Split the vanilla pod lengthwise and scrape out the seeds with a knife or spoon. Place the seeds and pod in a saucepan, then add the condensed milk and cream and bring to a boil.

Remove from the heat and strain the mixture through a sieve. The sieve should be large enough to let the vanilla seeds pass. Let the mixture cool slightly, then add the yoghurt and mix well.

Pour the mixture into a baking dish and bake in the water bath for about 30 to 40 minutes, depending on the size of the dish. The yoghurt should be slightly firm.

Let the yoghurt cool and then refrigerate to become completely firm.

CARAMELISED PINEAPPLE AND PINEAPPLE-CHILLI SORBET

MAURITIUS

YIELD
4 servings

LEVEL OF DIFFICULTY
Medium

TIME
4 hours

TAGS
Gluten-free, make ahead

CONTAINS
Chilli, dairy

Besides its beautiful beaches, Mauritius' iconic sugar cane fields are among the island's most memorable visual impressions.

As you can imagine, sugar has played an important role in the island's history, and still does. Besides ordinary refined, white sugar, there are a few less well known, artisanal varieties on the rise.

The most interesting is "muscovado", which is produced with the absolute minimal amount of physical processing. The cane juice is squeezed, heated and crystallised. No chemicals or bleaches are used, lending it a vastly different taste.

CHEF'S NOTE
To make your own pineapple puree, peel, core and chop a very ripe pineapple. Cook the pieces in a saucepan with a little sugar until soft. Then blend in a food processor until smooth. Freeze the mixture if you do not have an ice cream machine.

PINEAPPLE-CHILLI SORBET
75 ml (5 tablespoons) **water**
100 grams (½ cup) **sugar**
325 grams (1½ cups) **pineapple puree**
2 red chillies, very finely chopped

CARAMELISED PINEAPPLE
125 grams (¾ cup) **muscovado sugar**
20 grams (1½ tablespoons) **butter**
400 grams (14 oz) **pineapple**, peeled, cored and cubed
1 vanilla pod, halved, seeds scraped out

TO FINISH
10 ml (2 teaspoons) **rum**

PREPARATION
Heat the water and sugar in a saucepan to make a syrup. Add the pineapple puree and boil for five minutes.

Let the mass cool, then add the chilli and process in an ice cream machine to make the sorbet.

Melt the muscovado sugar over low to medium heat in a saucepan. Add the butter, pineapple and the vanilla pod and seeds and cook for about five minutes or until the pineapple absorbs the sugar.

To finish, add the rum and remove from the heat. Serve warm with the sorbet.

PAVLOVA
WITH WATTLESEEDS
AUSTRALIA

YIELD
1 cake

LEVEL OF DIFFICULTY
High

TIME
1 hour, 30 minutes

TAGS
Make ahead

CONTAINS
Dairy, egg, wheat

The wattle (acacia – the national flower of Australia) is an indigenous plant that grows wild all over the country. Its seeds were an important food source for the travelling native tribes of Australia.

While this native ingredient has long flown under the radar, it has recently been rediscovered and its great flavour, spice and texture have made it a growing favourite in modern Australian cuisine.

CHEF'S NOTES

You can substitute the wattleseeds with a mixture of hazelnut, chocolate and/or coffee. For this recipe, mix the whipped cream with five tablespoons of roasted ground hazelnuts, one teaspoon unsweetened cocoa powder and a pinch of salt. Or grate some tonka bean into the cream. You can make crunchy muesli by toasting oats in butter or oil.

PAVLOVA

4 egg whites
½ **lemon,** squeezed
1 teaspoon cornstarch
100 grams (⅓ cup) **sugar**
70 grams (½ cup) **crunchy muesli**
2 teaspoons aniseed powder

DRY WATTLE SEED POWDER

10 grams (4 tablespoons) **dry wattleseeds**
300 ml (1¼ cups) **cream,** whipped

PREPARATION

Heat the oven to 150° Celsius (300°F).

To make the "pavlova", use an electric mixer to whip the egg whites to a soft peak. While beating slowly, add the lemon juice, cornstarch and sugar. Continue whisking until the mass has stiff peaks, but be careful not to over-whisk. Line a baking tray with baking paper, spread the mixture with a spatula into a square, 1.5 cm (0.6 in) thick.

Bake the mass in the preheated oven for about 35 minutes (or less) until the cake begins to brown. The cake should not become too browned; it still needs to be soft to form a roll later. Remove the lightly browned cake from the oven and let cool and do not remove the baking paper.

To make the filling, soak the crushed dried wattleseeds for about 10 minutes in warm water to soften them. Strain the seeds and combine them with the whipped cream. Set aside.

Blend the muesli and aniseed powder in a food processor to make crumbs. When the cake is cooled, evenly distribute the crumbs in a thin layer over the cake. Use your hands to slightly press the crumbs into the cake. Flip the pavlova on a clean kitchen towel and remove the baking paper. Use a spatula to spread the wattleseed cream evenly on the cake.

Then using the towel, gently roll it into a roulade. Refrigerate the cake so that it becomes firm before serving. Serve chilled.

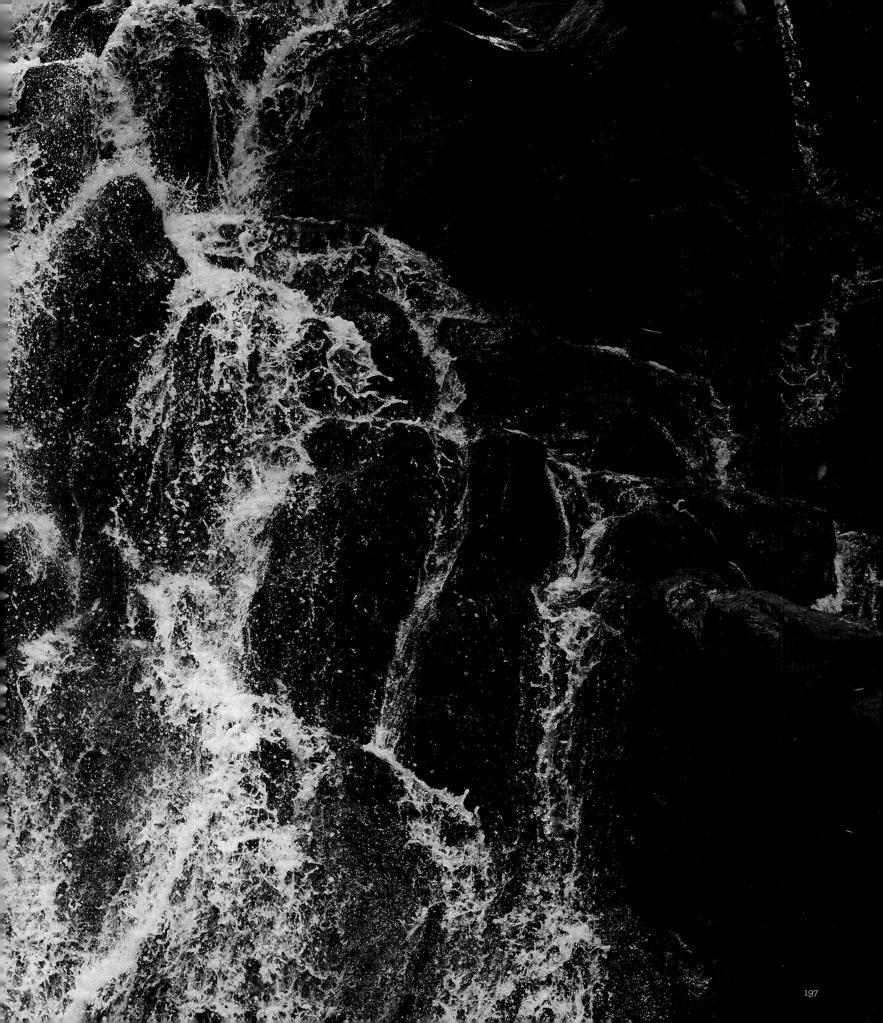

'LOOK DEEP INTO NATURE, AND THEN YOU WILL UNDERSTAND EVERYTHING BETTER'

Having a deep, respectful, and loving relationship with nature has always been a part of me, something that has defined me and nurtured my passion. I grew up in a small village in Austria and was surrounded by nature. We had no television or playroom; there was no community centre or playground. When we wanted to play, we went outside and played with sticks and stones, and let our imaginations be our guide.

At night, under blankets and with flashlights, we read books about cowboys and native Americans, knights and princesses, or about the adventures of pirates, Robin Hood and Huckleberry Finn. This fired our imaginations even more. We wanted to be the rebels in the woods, knights or adventurers and went deep into the forest and built forts and tree houses and spent entire days in our little world – far from adult supervision and organized playtimes. Sometimes – like Huck Finn – we carved a wooden branch into a fishing pole and tried to catch lunch at the pond, but invariably remained hungry.

So we started to secretly raid our grandmother's pantry and packed whatever we could get our hands on: sometimes items that we could eat raw, sometimes – because Granny grew suspicious – just ingredients. This is when we had to get creative or stay hungry, which of course was not an option.

Digging a pit, collecting wood and building a roaring campfire became a big part of our adventures and one of my early memories of preparing food – or at least what my personal perception of campfire food was. Soon, a simple sausage was no longer special enough and, since Robin Hood had once held spectacular feasts in the woods, I started to experiment. I discovered that different types of wood have different aromas, that some berries we found complemented one another in taste, or that resin is for more than just ruining clothes. I tried all sorts of things and found that I was quite good at it, and my friends seemed to be quite happy with the results as well.

I don't think I dreamed of becoming a chef back then, but I suppose my adventures in the Austrian woods gave me something far greater than a foundation for my passion. Growing up in the midst of nature subconsciously fuelled my desire to get off the beaten track and to be curious. It has helped me to remain within my comfort zone when I get lost in a village or city, or in the woods. It gave me the confidence to look closer and to question, but more importantly, to attempt to let fantasy be my guide.

I am driven by not knowing and the urge to find out, and I am aware that adventure awaits me and that discovery follows as a reward. After my years of travel, I began to realize what a precious and beautiful gift I carried within me.

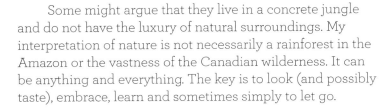

Some might argue that they live in a concrete jungle and do not have the luxury of natural surroundings. My interpretation of nature is not necessarily a rainforest in the Amazon or the vastness of the Canadian wilderness. It can be anything and everything. The key is to look (and possibly taste), embrace, learn and sometimes simply to let go.

All those beautiful sayings and motivational phrases – break the rules; get off the beaten track; think outside the box; do not accept the status quo; do not take 'no' for an answer – do not really mean much to me. These things come very naturally to me and I know that behind every door, behind every fence, behind every obstacle, there is something I can learn from, something that will inspire me!

So, go out and play!

INGREDIENTS

SERVING SIZES

For this book, we adjusted all recipes for home cooking. I assume that you will cook one, or perhaps several dishes together from this book. Many dishes can be served in combination with other dishes or as several consecutive courses. Note that if you serve one of these recipes as a single meal, people might eat several servings.

FINDING INGREDIENTS

Many ingredients can be found in Asian, Middle Eastern and speciality stores. Some spices can also be found in pharmacies. Ask your local Asian store about ingredients; if they do not stock them, they can probably order them for you. If you cannot find an ingredient in a shop, it can often be ordered online.

INGREDIENTS

Cooking oil: I leave the choice of cooking oil to you. It can be a vegetable or seed oil that is suitable for heating, such as sunflower, rapeseed (canola), soybean or olive oil. In a few cases, I recommend a specific oil (coconut oil, for example) for the flavour it adds to the dish. For deep-frying I recommend peanut oil or rice bran oil.

Salt: We use normal refined rock salt. I salt sparingly during the cooking process and like to season to taste at the end. I encourage you to do the same. Aquacasia cuisine is very flavourful and does not require heavy seasoning with salt and pepper.

Spices: Dried whole and ground spices are best stored in an airtight container in a dry, dark place. Spices do not go bad, but do lose their flavour over time. Curry leaves, kaffir lime leaves, galangal and ginger can be stored in the freezer.

Chilli: The varieties of chillies are endless and I encourage you to explore them all. Most commonly used in Mauritius and in this book is the long cayenne chilli. You might need to adjust the amount of chilli in the recipes to your taste and to the chilli you are using.

Garlic and onions: The garlic and onions of the Indian Ocean are somewhat milder than their European counterparts. Here, too, I recommend that you adjust the recipe to your taste.

Ginger: If you use organic ginger, you do not need to peel it. The best way to store ginger is whole and unpeeled in a resealable plastic bag, with the air sucked out, in the refrigerator.

TOOLS AND TECHNIQUES

TOOLS

Cooking utensils: Although we tried to do without too many utensils, certain ones are needed for specific recipes. The main cooking utensils used in this book are a precise scale, a mortar and pestle, electric food processor, stand mixer and hand blender. The most important tools, of course, are a sharp knife and a large chopping board that does not slide on the work surface (to prevent this use sealing gaskets).

Mortar and pestle: We use a mortar and pestle for grinding and crushing ingredients for pastes. Alternatively, you can use an electric food processor.

Chopper: I do not mention a mini-chopper in the recipes, but you can use an electric mini-chopper to assist you with chopping ingredients such as garlic, ginger and onions.

TECHNIQUES

Sweating off: This technique is the opposite of stir-frying. On low heat, the food is cooked slowly, which creates a flavour base for the dish.

Sautéing: The food is cooked in a hot pan with oil while stirring. This method lies between sweating off and stir-frying.

Stir-frying: The food is cooked on a smoking hot metal surface with just enough oil to coat it while constantly stirring to ensure even cooking and to prevent burning.

Deep-frying: The food is fully immersed in hot oil (160 - 190° Celsius (325 - 375° F). It is essential to get the size of the pieces and the heat right so that the food is cooked through by the time the surface turns golden brown. If you do not own a deep-fryer, you can fry in a small saucepan.

MAIN INDEX

COUNTRY INDEX

FISH & SEAFOOD (FI)
MEAT & POULTRY (ME)
SPICE MIX & RUBS (SP)
SIDES (SI)
SNACKS (SN)
SWEETS (SW)

FEATURED COUNTRIES

WESTERN AUSTRALIA
Multicultural and spiced with fresh Pacific Rim ingredients and multicultural fusion plates.

COMOROS
The charming residents of Comoros are descended from Arab merchants, Persian aristocrats, African slaves and Portuguese explorers.

INDONESIA
A country of many cultures, traditions and foods, it is as if 50 countries have melted into one. A veritable paradise for foodies.

MADAGASCAR
Astoundingly diverse and unspoilt; the remarkable fauna and flora are matched by breathtaking surroundings and amazing street food.

MALDIVES
The Maldives is one of the world's most geographically dispersed countries. This chain of 26 atolls – nearly 1200 islands – spreads over roughly 90,000 square kilometres (35,000 square miles).

MAURITIUS
The real Mauritius is a hot curry mix of different cultures, scents and picturesque fishing villages. Mark Twain once wrote that "Mauritius was made first – then heaven, being copied after Mauritius". Heaven, we hope, comes with a kitchen.

RÉUNION
Réunion has a fascinating Creole, African, Indian, Chinese and French heritage, with a wealth of culinary treasures.

SEYCHELLES
If you are looking for more than a suntan, the Seychelles offer a myriad of fantastic inspirations.

SRI LANKA
Sri Lanka is spectacular with its 2000 years of culture, some of the most charming people on the planet and its amazing little dishes. A jewel awaiting discovery.

ACKNOWLEDGEMENTS

WE, THE TEAM AT SHANTI MAURICE, A NIRA RESORT, WOULD LIKE TO EXPRESS
OUR SINCERE APPRECIATION FOR YOUR GENEROSITY AND SUPPORT.

Thank you to all who opend their doors and pockets to support this book,
those who have been believers and supporters from day one
and for understanding our vision.

LA GIRONDELLE

 CharteredBrokersGroup

QUINCAILLERIE MANIC   STV DISTRIBUTERS   TIME TRAVELLERS

CREDITS

Photography by Lukas Lienhard
Authors W. Reinbacher, D. Accola, T. Evill
Recipe Testing & Editing by Laura Schälchli
Editing by Michael Johnson, Zurich

Concept by MPS Puri
Produced & Designed by D. Accola for Confused Communications LLC

Special thanks to: Guido Farina, Rakesh Bhowany & Team, Ricardo Samuel &
Team, Vikash Toofany, Deepak Balgobin, Anuradha, Julien, Sonny, Lotide and
everyone at Shanti Maurice, Jack (†2016), Chocolateman and the
friendly people of the Indian Ocean

Printed in Germany (Climate Neutral)
by Offset Druckerei Grammlich

1st edition is limited to 3,000 copies

First published in 2016
Chinese   Year of the Fire Monkey
Buddhist 2559
Hebrew   5776
Indian   1938
Islamic   1437
Persian   1395

ISBN 978-99949-0-211-8